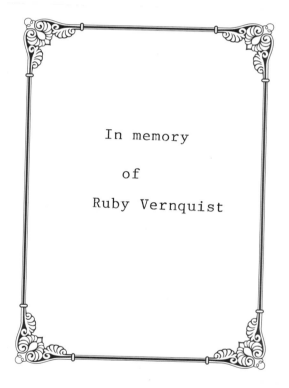

In memory

of

Ruby Vernquist

The White House
in Miniature

The White House
IN MINIATURE

**Based on the White House Replica by
John, Jan, and the Zweifel Family**

Gail Buckland

Photographs by Kathleen Culbert-Aguilar

W. W. Norton & Company
New York · London

First Edition

The text of this book is composed in Sabon
with the display set in Gill Sans.
Manufactured by Arnoldo Mondadori Editore, Verona, Italy
Book design by Katy Homans

Library of Congress Cataloging-in-Publication Data
Buckland, Gail.
The White House in miniature : based on the
White House replica by John, Jan and the Zweifel family
Zweifel / Gail Buckland ; photographs by
Kathleen Culbert-Aquilar
p.   cm.
1. Zweifel, John. 2. Zweifel, Jan.
3. White House (Washington, D.C.)
4. Historical buildings—Washington (D.C.)—Models.
I. Culbert-Aguilar, Kathleen. II. Title.
NK8473.5.Z94B83 1994
725'.17'09753—dc20   94-4193

ISBN 0-393-03663-4
Printed in Italy
W. W. Norton & Company, Inc.
500 Fifth Avenue , New York, NY 10110
W. W. Norton & Company Ltd.
10 Coptic Street , London WC1A 1PU

1 2 3 4 5 6 7 8 9 0

page i: The windows on the first floor of the White House have
alternating triangular and arched stone pediments supported by
large consoles. Beneath the sills are bands of interlocking circles
(guilloche). The second-floor windows have acanthus leaf brackets
supporting the sills.

page ii: Kevin Buckland, age 9, peeking through the doorway
of the Red Room.

For Barry, with love

Contents

137979

Foreword

A Welcome from Former President and Mrs. Gerald Ford

It is our very special pleasure to welcome you to the White House Replica. We had the honor and privilege to live in the White House during our country's bicentennial. The White House Replica, created as a gift to the nation on its two-hundredth birthday, was one of the most exciting projects to have emerged from the celebrations.

The White House is owned by all Americans, but only a small number ever have the opportunity to visit in person this great house of American history. John and Jan Zweifel wanted to recreate the home of the president and first lady in order to take it to people, in all fifty states, who could not come to Washington themselves. We were delighted that while residing at 1600 Pennsylvania Avenue, we could be of assistance to them. Our initial trust in their creative skills and patriotism has been amply rewarded. Many, many millions more Americans and foreign friends have "seen" the White House because of their splendid miniaturization.

The White House is a living symbol of the United States of America and the home of first families since 1800. Its unique history instills pride in our country's democratic heritage. To come to the White House, or behold the Zweifels' meticulous representation of the rooms, helps us to better understand our nation's past and feel a sense of continuity with it. May the White House continue to inspire us, our children, and our children's children—until the tricentennial, and beyond.

Gerald and Betty Ford

The 1-inch-to-1-foot scale model of President Ford's Oval Office.

Preface

The White House in Miniature is a significant contribution to our heritage. Although well over a million people tour the White House annually, most Americans will never have the opportunity to visit our nation's capital. For many of our citizens, this beautiful and faithful reproduction of the White House is the only means of fully visualizing the home of the President of the United States.

Jacqueline Kennedy, in the first White House guidebook, wrote for the introduction, "It [the guide] was planned—at first—for children. . . . Its purpose was to stimulate their sense of history and pride in their country." The White House in Miniature, though conceived for adults, captures the imagination of the young to as great a degree as adults.

I have known Jan and John Zweifel for more than thirty years and I have been pleased to assist in their project for over twenty years. I have the greatest admiration for their talent and perseverance. The Zweifels share with their artistic children a love for their country and a very special affection for the White House. It is this love and affection that made it possible for them to devote the time, talent, and finances required to create the White House in Miniature. In 1992, the 200th anniversary year of the White House cornerstone-laying ceremony, the White House in Miniature was on display at the Smithsonian Institution's Museum of American History. Approximately four million people took advantage of the opportunity to see it—a far greater number than was able to visit the 1600 Pennsylvania Avenue White House.

All Americans owe a debt of gratitude to the Zweifel family. The White House in Miniature is a magnificent gift to the nation. Like the White House itself, the miniature transcends politics and personalities and is to be shared with all of our citizens.

Rex W. Scouten
Curator
The White House

The White House replica (including the two wings) is over 60 feet long and 20 feet wide. It weighs 10 tons. Regardless, it has been exhibited in all fifty states and in Europe and Japan. Approximately 43 million people have seen it. The Zweifels have been working on the replica, originally called "The Hand-Carved White House in Miniature," for over thirty years.

Acknowledgments

In 1961 John F. Kennedy summoned Americans to ask not what their country could do for them, but what they could do for their country. John and Jan Zweifel responded by giving to the nation an unparalleled gift. Without the Zweifel family's years of dedication to their project, there would be no model White House and no book. I not only applaud their remarkable achievement but also appreciate their assistance with the research and photography required to complete this book.

Rex Scouten served his country years before Kennedy's call, and serves it still. He was a Secret Service agent for Presidents Truman and Eisenhower; an assistant to and later chief usher for Eisenhower, Kennedy, Johnson, Nixon, Ford, Carter, and Reagan; and, more recently, White House curator for Presidents Bush and Clinton. It is with respect and admiration that I thank Mr. Scouten for writing the Preface and for kindly reading the manuscript. He knows the White House—its history, lore, logistics, and layout—better than anyone.

Kathleen Culbert-Aguilar did an exceptional job of photographing a technically complicated subject under often difficult circumstances. I thank her for not only her professionalism but also her good will and generosity of spirit. Gerald Matthess (who never said no and can fix anything), Robert Wherrett, Joyce Hutching, Diane Graham-Henry, and José Aguilar—all helped with the photography, usually till dawn's early light, as did Giedre Andrasiumaite and Kevin and Alaina Buckland when parts of the display were in Westfield, New Jersey. Their help is deeply appreciated.

Most of the photography took place while the replica was on exhibit at the John F. Kennedy Presidential Library in Boston, Massachusetts. Mr. Charles Daly, director, and his staff welcomed us and facilitated our work. I would especially like to acknowledge the support of Amy Forman, Brad Gerratt, Alan Goodrich, Frank Rigg, and Captain Ernest Biancuzzo and his courteous security guards.

Anitra Dawson, Bill and Phyllis Dye, Helen Hartcorn, Barbara Meyers, Gary Nixon, Judith G. Ohanian, and Robert Robinson are skilled craftspeople who have made major contributions to the replica and have shared their memories, insights, and know-how with me.

The historian Kevin Baker read the manuscript and offered many helpful suggestions. Russell H. Armentrout; Charles ("Chappie") Fox; Steven Heller of the *New York Times*; Milton Mitler of the U.S. Chamber of Commerce; Mrs. Roland Roberts; Rob and Margery Robinson; Dr. William Seale; Elliot Sivowitch of the Division of Electricity, Smithsonian Institution; Ambassador Andreas A. M. VanAgt; Gary L. Walters, chief usher at the White House; and Nancy Yoder all made contributions that helped in the writing of the text.

Sarah Connolly and her daughter Dorothy Zarba; Pat Dorsey at the Harry S. Truman Presidential Library; Arthur Elias; Natalie and Lorimer Miller; and Donald B. Schewe, director of the Jimmy Carter Presidential Library, all lent objects used in the scale photographs.

Wayne Blankenbeckler was the photographer with the Zweifels in August 1975 when the main research in the White House took place. I thank him for permission to reproduce his photographs taken at

John, Jan, and Jack Zweifel showing President Gerald Ford his miniaturized Oval Office during a visit to his home in Rancho Mirage, California, February 15, 1982.

the time. Tony Auth, political cartoonist, of the *Philadelphia Inquirer*, kindly gave permission for the use of his drawing of Gerald Ford. Martin Silverstein, director of photography at CBS, provided the still from Mrs. Kennedy's television tour of the White House. Bruce Bonnet made the photograph of the Zweifel family in 1990.

Hardly a page of my historical text has not been informed and enhanced by the scholarship and writings of Dr. William Seale. His books on the White House are authoritative, lucid, and show a profound understanding of American history. Dr. William Kloss's *A Nation's Pride: Art in the White House* has provided numerous anecdotes and insights into the works that have graced the walls of our presidents' home. Margaret Klaphor's articles and books, especially about White House entertaining, have helped bring both the house and its occupants to life.

The skilled and supportive professionals at Norton—Starling Lawrence, my editor; Nancy Palmquist, project editor; Susan Gaustad, copyeditor; and Andy Marasia, production manager—all helped guide, shape, and improve the book. I deeply appreciate their efforts. My literary agent Robert Ducas was the first person to say "Do it!" and I thank him for his confidence, conviction, and counsel.

A special note of appreciation goes to Katy Homans. She designed the book with sensitivity and discernment, her enthusiasm for the visual and written material was heartening, and her advice invaluable.

My husband, Barry, and my children, Alaina and Kevin, are wonderfully and consistently supportive. Their love, understanding, and vitality is beyond my ability to properly acknowledge.   —G.B.

Note from John and Jan Zweifel

We asked President Ford to help us give the White House to the people. He concurred and opened "the big door" so that we could do the research that had never before been allowed or encouraged. He is patriotic, congenial, and a passionate supporter of the rights of the individual. Without his and Mrs. Ford's help, we could not have made the miniature.

For always trusting and encouraging us, we want to extend our heartfelt thanks to Rex Scouten. He is both deacon and trustee to the house; he is the angel who looks over it and makes not only us, but everyone, welcome.

We thank our six children—Jack, James, Kathryn, Ray, Janet, and Julie—for their endless help and support; John's parents, Kathryn and Earl Zweifel, and Jan's parents, Helen and Ed Cleary, for understanding our obsession; and John's grandparents, Lillian and Ray ("Spot") Young, for the things they taught us about art and life.

The Zweifels would also like to thank Donald Rumsfeld, the late Dr. Theodore Marrs, and Richard Cheney, all one-time assistants to President Ford; Gerald Matthess for his enthusiasm and loyalty; and Gwen Dycus for her patriotic patience.

Introduction

A fascination with either the reduction or enlargement of an object is not uncommon. There are thousands of handmade objects, commercial products, and literary allusions that exploit our interest in the transformation of a familiar commodity into either a giant or dwarf reincarnation of itself—the matchbox car, the super Crayola, tin soldiers, Alice, Gulliver, teddy bears, model boats, to name but a few.

What is nearly incomprehensible, and at the very heart of John, Jan, and Jack Zweifel's scale model of the White House, is the time spent researching, executing, and maintaining it. Hour after hour, day after day, year after year, decade after decade, and an anticipated lifetime after lifetime have been given over to making the model an exact replica of the real White House. It is a never-ending avocation. After countless days and nights, a chair or chandelier or table may be completed, but then the paintings in the state rooms are switched, there is a new acquisition, an oriental carpet is replaced, a president is elected, the Oval Office is rearranged. The work never stops. There are always more details of "our White House" to show the American people.

A burnt-out light bulb, the size of a grain of rice, can take five hours to change. One volunteer worked ten years on a petit point rug for the diminutive Blue Room, only to learn that the original upon which it is based was to be replaced. In any miniaturization,

craftsmanship, proportion, and illusion are fundamental components. In the White House replica, a fourth has equal importance: fidelity. Whimsy and wish, which motivated many of the makers of the world's great dollhouses, have no place in the "Hand Carved White House in Miniature."

The White House replica was conceived as "a gift to the people, from the people." For over thirty years, John Zweifel, the driving force behind the project, has not rested. Always demanding of himself, he coaxes his wife, Jan, commandeers his family and friends, organizes volunteers all over the United States, hires skilled craftspeople, and inspires them all to try that much harder, redo anything flawed or less than ideal, and add to the miniature, object by object, room by room. Never completed, always evolving, the White House replica is in a constant state of "becoming."

Presidents realize that their lease on 1600 Pennsylvania Avenue is short-term, even when they act as though they are firmly entrenched. The public often forgets that the White House is theirs, not the current occupant's. During a White House garden party in the 1850s, a guest approached President Franklin Pierce and inquired: "Mr. President, can't I go through your fine house? I've heard so much about it that I'd give a great deal to see it." The president responded: "Why my dear sir, that is not *my* house. It's the people's house! You shall certainly go through it if you wish."[1] The second Franklin to live in the house, far better loved and remembered, shared the same sentiment. Roosevelt said: "I never forget that I live in a house owned by all the American people." "It is public," wrote the journalist "Olivia" in 1870 about the White House. "It belongs to the people. When we go to the

The composition combines a 1941 console radio, a six-cent Roosevelt stamp, a dime, and from the replica's Diplomatic Reception Room (the room in which Franklin Delano Roosevelt delivered his fireside chats) an easy chair, a secretary-bookcase, a side chair, and the carpet made by miniaturist Anitra Dawson displaying all the state seals.

Executive Mansion we go to our own house."[2] The Zweifels' goal has always been to give 1600 Pennsylvania Avenue back to the people. If the people can't have a key, they can at least have a peek.

No "normal" person could have achieved what John Zweifel with the help of his wife, his six children (especially Jack), and his thousands of volunteers and craftspeople have accomplished. Over 500,000 man hours were spent constructing the miniature White House, and tens of millions (the estimate is 43 million) of people have stood in front of the replica spellbound. "Unbelievable" is the usual response, because no one can imagine that a copy of the White House in such detail is feasible. Yes, they can believe a Hollywood-like set is possible, suggestive of rooms and decor. But exact? Down to the switches on the walls and electrical outlets; French Empire clocks and early-nineteenth-century mantels, moldings, and cornices; knickknacks and priceless antiques; John Adams' coffee urn and hanging floral baskets; personal items on the president's desk and discarded notes in the wastepaper baskets in the Calligraphers' Office? No, this can't be possible, yet here it is, in minute and munificent detail.

John Zweifel says the research takes longer than the actual fabrication, in large part because the research involves encounters with Washington bureaucracy. First given permission to build a model White House by the Kennedy administration in 1962, the Zweifels were not allowed to take the necessary measurements and photographs inside the house until 1975. Nevertheless, they worked consistently over those intervening years, using photographs, published drawings, and their memories from frequent public tours. They did not know if the wee furniture they were carving would have the verisimilitude required to make their recreation an *exact* miniaturized copy of the original. Zweifel's patience and persistence in

his life's work have been phenomenal. The White House replica, made by many, is nevertheless the product of one man's initiative, vision, skill, and determination.

If the researching and the actual making of the 1-inch-to-1-foot scale model stretches the imagination, the second part of Zweifel's ambition is unfathomable. Reason would demand that once assembled, the miniature White House lie in state like, for example, Queen Mary's Dolls' House at Windsor Castle. But Zweifel took this 60-foot-long and 20-foot-wide, 10-ton, million-dollar "baby" on the road, visiting all fifty states and a few foreign countries. His aim: to take the White House to the people, as most people will never be able to visit Washington, D.C. (The itinerary the replica followed from 1975 to the present is given on pages 195–201.) There are hundreds of minuscule, fragile objects that must be individually and carefully wrapped each time the replica moves. And Zweifel did this, during the mid-1970s to 1980, repeatedly.

Each individual surveying the White House replica experiences it first in a personal way based on his or her own enthusiasms or knowledge and then in a more general, collective manner. One might be initially impressed by the fine eighteenth-century architecture or be thrilled at finding famous rooms or spaces such as the Oval Office, Rose Garden, or East Room. Someone else may at first be overwhelmed by the craftsmanship and magnitude of the display. Another individual may be mesmerized by the working mini-televisions or surprised to find even the president's pet included. Many people become reflective, thinking about the men and women whose moments of greatness, and sometimes defeat, transpired within these walls. Eventually, though, all visitors looking into the open rooms on the south side become giddy with the feeling that they are seeing something they are not quite supposed to see, or thought they never could see in its entirety. And this abundance of color, lights, and detail is counterbalanced by the clean white architectural lines of the north side, which quiet the crowds and make most Americans feel reverence for this venerable old building.

The White House is a symbol not of power but of authority vested in an elected representative of the people. The people decide who will hold the four-year lease. The White House is a beacon of democracy, evidence of the peaceful transition of leadership from one chosen citizen to another. A visit to the exhibit or a look through the pages of this book is a once-in-a-lifetime, VIP tour of this great house of American history, where every president and first lady except George and Martha Washington have lived.

The only permanent resident of 1600 Pennsylvania Avenue is the democratic ideal; the politicians are only passing through. The United States has a common home that any boy or girl can aspire to, whose rooms have hosted and been home to giants, the likes of Jefferson and Lincoln, as well as lesser men and women. John Adams, the first president to live in the White House, wrote to his wife, Abigail, on the first full day of his residence: "I pray Heaven to bestow the best of blessings on this house, and on all that shall hereafter inhabit it. May none but honest and wise men ever rule under this roof!" The house the Zweifels have given to the American people is the idealized house of Adams' benediction, not the con-

troversial battleground discussed daily in the news. The Zweifels have successfully depoliticized the building and presented it as the most notable and celebrated house—past, present, and future—in the nation and the world.

The story of the making and exhibiting of the White House replica is a tale of the Zweifels' patriotism, obsession, frustration, endurance, skill, setbacks, and ultimately satisfaction. It is also a story about their hope. Not simply the hope that each administration will support the project or that the tiny furniture packed in the back of a tractor-trailer will not break on the long, bumpy journeys or that a craftsperson can carve a chair leg correctly on the third rather than thirtieth attempt, but the hope that one family, an "average family," can make a difference in how people view the White House and consequently their country.

The chapter entitled "A Gift to the People" touches upon some of the drama and some of the hardship of this saga. The text and extended captions accompanying the photographs provide narratives for each historic room and descriptions of the furnishings. The magic and enchantment on the following pages rests in the Zweifels' creation and the dazzling photographs by Kathleen Culbert-Aguilar.

Gail Buckland
Westfield, New Jersey
April 1994

North Side, Pennsylvania Avenue view

East Wing   East Colonnade   North Front and Por

South Side

Executive Offices (West Wing)   Oval Office and Patio   Rose Garden and Press Briefing Room   Cut-away, South Fr

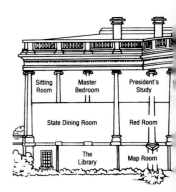

Sitting Room | Master Bedroom | President's Study

State Dining Room | Red Room

The Library | Map Room

West Colonnade   West Wing

Jacqueline Kennedy Garden and Movie Theater   Administrative Offices (East Wing)

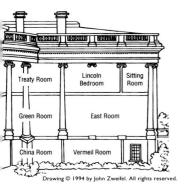

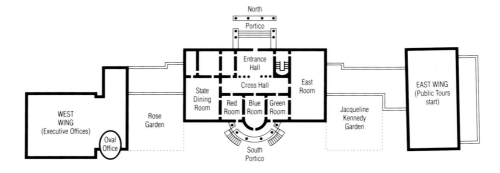

Please Come In

The book, only 1 inch high, is a miniaturized reprint of *Reagan: The Man from Main Street USA* by Vance H. Trimble (1980). With a magnifying glass, the text and illustrations by Jack Gold are legible. The picture over the fireplace is a diminutive copy of *The Cincinnati Enquirer* by William M. Harnett (1888), a master of trompe l'oeil painting.

The Library

Abigail Adams hanging laundry to dry in the East Room is a well-known anecdote of American history. Where clothes were washed is a better-kept secret. In 1800, John and Abigail Adams, the first occupants of the White House, assigned this ground- (or basement-) level room for laundry and storage, luxuries such as libraries having no place in the still-unfinished, fiercely cold and damp, unfurnished president's house. The progression from laundry to library would have pleased the second president, who once said that he studied politics and war so that his "sons may have the liberty" to learn mathematics, philosophy, geography, natural history, naval architecture, navigation, commerce, and agriculture, in order to give their own children "a right to study Painting, Poetry, Musick, Architecture, Statuary, Tapestry and Porcelaine."

In the actual White House, the Library is located on the northeast side of the house, opposite the Vermeil Room. In order to make it visible to viewers of the replica, it is shown in the southwest corner of the ground floor in the area occupied by the White House physician in the real White House. (This is the only room in the replica not accurately situated.) From Teddy Roosevelt's administration to about 1920, this space was a men's lounge with adjoining toilet facilities. It was then used by the servants and for storage, and progressively became more dilapidated until the next Roosevelt decided the White House should have a library.

The first occupant to be distressed to find the White House without a proper library was actually Abigail Fillmore, wife of the thirteenth president. She and her husband, like Bill and Hillary Clinton, loved to be surrounded by books, and within a month of

The two Indian portraits on the right wall were painted about 1822 by Charles Bird King as part of a commission from the Archives of the American Indian, Washington's first museum. That year Hayne Hudjihini, or "Eagle of Delight," of the Oto tribe (top painting) and Sharitarish, or "Wicked Chief," of the Pawnee tribe (bottom painting) visited Washington and "the Great Father," President Monroe, as part of a seventeen Indian delegation from the powerful and militant tribes of the Great Plains. They had been invited by Secretary of War John C. Calhoun, who hoped to convince the Indians that resistance to the U.S. government was useless and unwise. They were formally received by President Monroe in the Red Room on February 4, 1822.

Monroe's offer to send missionaries to instruct the Indians in Christianity and agriculture was refused. The chiefs said they preferred their own life of trapping beaver and hunting buffalo, and Sharitarish added: "We have plenty of land, if you will keep your people off it." He also added, after the Indians had presented Monroe with traditional Native American gifts, that he hoped the president would have the presents kept "in some conspicuous part of your lodge, so that when we are gone . . . if our children should visit this place, as we do now, they may see and recognize with pleasure the deposits of their fathers, and reflect on the times that are past."[3] The gifts were lost long ago. Hayne Hudjihini contracted measles during her visit and died soon after returning home.

The replica of the New England Sheraton-style armchair, also known as a lolling or "Martha Washington" type, is seen atop volume 2 of William Seale's *The President's House*, a book measuring 6 by 9 inches.

Millard Fillmore's taking office in 1850, bookshelves were being constructed to conform to the curved walls of what is now the Yellow Oval Room on the second floor. And to the Fillmores' delight, Congress appropriated $2,000 for books to be purchased under the president's direction, but as William Seale, the distinguished White House historian notes, "It was generally assumed that the one in charge would be his wife." By 1929, however, the Oval Room had come to be used for other purposes and the White House collection of books was in the corridor.

Franklin Roosevelt wanted a proper library and cast his eye on many of the underutilized, poorly maintained rooms on the ground level. In the spring of 1935, he asked his architect, Lorenzo Winslow, to push his wheelchair to the basement and give an opinion on the suitability of the northeast corner chamber. Winslow thought it would make a fine library and was soon drawing up plans to submit to the president.

Winslow would spend far more time in this 500-square-foot room than he ever imagined. On Sunday, December 7, 1941, just hours after the Japanese bombed Pearl Harbor, Roosevelt called Winslow to the White House to discuss turning the Library into the White House architectural office; the president needed blueprints for a new office complex at the White House to accommodate the emergency staff. Even with the onset of war, Roosevelt wanted the architect close at hand in order to keep an eye on the drawings and to voice his approval or dissent. The East Wing was born at this time.

By 1961, the Library was ready not for redecoration, a word First Lady Jacqueline Kennedy abhorred, but for restoration. According to her White House secretary, Mary Gallagher, Henry Francis du Pont provided Mrs. Kennedy with Thomas Jefferson's guidelines on choosing appropriate furnishings for a library and on "the appearance and selection of

books." In the September 1, 1961, issue of *Life* magazine, Mrs. Kennedy is quoted as saying, "We took out the Agatha Christie and, following the suggestion of the historian Julian Boyd, brought in the writings of American Presidents and other books by writers who had influenced American history, such as Thomas Paine."

The Library is an example of a "painted room" of the early nineteenth century. An elegant room, more intimate than the state rooms on the first floor, the Library is often used for interviews, tapings, and small teas; it is also the location of the gentlemen's lounge.

The Library, done in the Federal style, contains a set of caned furniture attributed to Duncan Phyfe, the renowned cabinetmaker who led a large and distinguished workshop in New York from 1800 to 1820. The wood paneling in the room was cut from timbers removed from the interior of the White House during the renovation that took place in 1948–52 and is painted in a manner reflective of the early nineteenth century.

Above the Duncan Phyfe mahogany drum table (c. 1810–15), in the center of the room is a painted wood and cut glass chandelier (c. 1800) that hung in the house once owned by James Fenimore Cooper, author of *The Last of the Mohicans*. The neoclassical mantel (c. 1795–1805), decorated with grape-leaf swags and bellflower pendants, was removed from a house in Salem, Massachusetts. The drapery of strié silk with flambé stripe is one of the most attractive fabrics in the White House.

The Library contains 2,700 volumes pertaining mostly to American life, and papers of and works by former presidents. Robert C. Robinson, who for five years spent between five and six weeks a year as a volunteer working on the White House replica, said he was most proud of the 2,250 miniature books that he made, "some leaning one way, some another. Some lying flat and open to read. Most of them for the Library."

The Chippendale furniture gives the Map Room its distinct appearance among White House rooms. The pieces are some of the finest examples in the United States of this style of furniture, fashionable in the second half of the eighteenth century. The stately, elaborately carved Chippendale highboy made in Philadelphia stands sentinel to the right of Rembrandt Peale's portrait of Thomas Jefferson, the best-known likeness of the third president. (President William Jefferson Clinton has moved the portrait to a place of honor in the Blue Room, the principal reception room of the White House.)

Another founding father, and equally revered, keeps Jefferson company. Benjamin Franklin's portrait by Benjamin Wilson is in the foreground on the left of the photograph, above the blockfront desk. The painting, which hung in Franklin's home in Philadelphia, was removed by the British officer John André during the American Revolution. André was later hung as a spy for assisting Bene-

dict Arnold. His commanding officer, General Charles Grey (later Earl Grey), took the painting back to England. In 1906, the fourth Earl Grey returned the portrait in honor of the bicentennial of Franklin's birth. Franklin's own feeling about the theft of his portrait in 1778 was that it left the painting's "companion, my wife, by itself a kind of widow" on the wall. (The portrait is now in Clinton's private office in the family quarters.)

Map Room

The miniature rug in the photograph is 17 by 24 inches. Like everything in the miniature White House, it was done 1-inch-to-the-foot, but reducing a nineteenth-century Heriz rug and keeping faithful to color and design is a mammoth task for such tiny stitches. Helen Hartcorn, who made the rug, still has the calluses to prove it. A regular size needlepoint needle and a skein of wool, actually used in making the carpet, show just how small the stitches are.

Between 1902 and 1941, ladies powdered their noses and arranged their hair in this ground-floor chamber before ascending the stairs to the state rooms on the first floor. From January 1942 until the end of World War II, military maneuvers and information concerning the fate of millions was kept guarded within the confines of these walls. For here, two stories directly below his bedroom, Franklin Delano Roosevelt set up his war room. The most confidential materials were kept on file, including all war-related correspondence from Churchill, Stalin, and Chiang Kai-shek.

During World War II, the Map Room was strictly a military operation within the White House. Surprisingly, it was a movie star who was most instrumental in helping set it up. Lieutenant Henry Montgomery, better known as Robert Montgomery, was for several weeks an observer in Churchill's Map Room in London. When he was called on to help with the White House Map Room, at the time of Pearl Harbor, there was only a globe in the Oval Office, a globe in the president's study, and a set of maps the president used principally for his stamp collection. Montgomery recognized that the president needed large-scale charts of the Pacific and Atlantic and more modest-size charts of all other combat zones.

The one doorway had a "No Admittance" sign and a sentry posted twenty-four hours a day. After a time, even Eleanor was barred (although she barged past the guard on a few occasions). Six men from the army and six from the navy were posted here, their responsibility being to keep all the president's military papers organized and the placement of troops current on the maps covering the walls. Ships, airplanes, and troops were identified by different-colored pins and were constantly being repositioned. The three Allied leaders, identified with pins in the shape of a cigarette holder (Roosevelt), a cigar (Churchill), and a briar pipe (Stalin), were also tracked.

There was another peculiar pin, one that perhaps was just the tiniest compensation for the burdens of serving as commander in chief. It marked the ship on which Franklin Jr. served and was, according to an officer who worked in the Map Room, the one FDR always looked at first upon entering the room. Roosevelt stopped at the Map Room generally twice daily until ill health in 1944 required that the Map Room be brought to him.

In the early 1960s, the room was returned to the ladies, but only temporarily. Portraits of first ladies were hung on the walls, overseeing, so to speak, the work of the White House's first curator, Mrs. John Newton Pearce. In 1970, the room was redecorated in the Chippendale style to serve as a reception room.

Diplomatic Reception Room

"I want to talk for a few minutes with the people of the United States about banking," proposed Franklin Delano Roosevelt from a chair in the Diplomatic Reception Room just eight days after taking office in 1933. Without raising his voice, he was heard by millions. From that day until his death, FDR entered the homes and hearts of Americans via radio waves emanating from the former servants' quarters of the executive mansion. And through the same powerful conductor, Americans were transported emotionally to the White House, where, throughout the Great Depression and World War II, they and the president considered the problems of state.

No matter that the fireplace in the room where the famous fireside chats were broadcast was a fake (later to be a functioning hearth); the president radi-

The distinctive wallpaper was printed with over 1,600 woodblocks on small sheets of paper, which were then glued together into panels. It was made by Jean Zuber and Company of Rixheim, Alsace, France, in about 1834 and is titled "Scenic America" or "Views of North America." The sites, all particularly admired by Europeans, were based on engravings from the 1820s. The panels show New York from Weehawken, New Jersey; the U.S. Military Academy at West Point; Boston Harbor; Winnebago Indians; the Natural Bridge of Virginia; a horse-drawn rail coach; and Niagara Falls from the Canadian side.

The wallpaper was originally at the Stoner House in Thurmont, Maryland, where it caught the eye of Mrs. Kennedy. It was taken down rather hurriedly in 1961 and arrived at the White House looking somewhat like a jigsaw puzzle that then had to be carefully reassembled. The National Society of Interior Designers provided the funds, but Mrs. Kennedy was criticized, nevertheless, for what some considered extravagance. Her choice of the vintage wallpaper for the Diplomatic Reception Room was inspired, and her acquisitions for the White House never did cost taxpayers anything.

Desks and bookcases in early American homes were symbols of their owners' mercantile and intellectual prowess, a "fusion of commerce and culture," in the words of Morrison Heckscher, curator of American decorative arts at the Metropolitan Museum of Art in New York. They were the most costly and important piece of household furniture. The mahogany secretary-bookcase on the west wall of the Diplomatic Reception Room dates from 1797 and was made by John Shaw, a cabinetmaker who crafted furniture for the Maryland legislature. The settee is of mahogany and cane, made in New York about 1800, possibly by Abraham Slover and

Jacob Taylor. The splats form Gothic arches in back. To the left of the secretary-bookcase is a window seat, one of a pair attributed to the New York workshop of Duncan Phyfe (c. 1810–15).

Factual information about the miniature rug made by Anitra Dawson:
3¹/₂ years of stitching, average 4 to 5 hours a day
900 stitches to the square inch
22 x 32 inches oval
a couple million stitches

28

ated his own warmth. The broadcasts coming from the White House were assuring. As William Seale notes: "It is significant that [FDR] set his fireside chats in the White House. By making a point of being there, the President evoked a rich sense of continuity that linked the old house to the Founding Fathers." In times of trouble, it was crucial that the American people honored their past and had a sense of their destiny.

The Diplomatic Reception Room was transformed from a servants' hall in the early 1800s to a boiler room (the first central heating was installed under Martin Van Buren in 1837), to broadcast room under Roosevelt and Truman, and finally to the main entrance and exit for the president and his family. It is here, too, that ambassadors arrive to present their credentials to the president. Teddy Roosevelt's architect, Charles McKim, was the first to realize the architectural splendor of the basement level with the groin vaulting in the central corridor and its third "oval" room opening directly to the south lawn.

In the photograph on pages 26–27, a miniaturization of Gilbert Stuart's celebrated painting of George Washington oversees the activities of the Diplomatic Reception Room from its honorary position over the famous fireplace. Under President and Mrs. Eisenhower, this was the first room in the White House decorated entirely with American antiques appropriate to the age and traditions of the house. The Federal furniture (1780–1810) was a gift from the American Institute of Interior Designers. Jacqueline Kennedy left the furniture in place and gave the room its unique resplendence by adding the nineteenth-century French wallpaper showing early American scenes.

During his 1952 television tour of the White House after a renovation that had taken four years, Harry Truman passed through the Diplomatic Reception Room talking about its history and some of the changes he had made. The one he wanted the TV audience to note especially was the removal of the presidential seal from the floor of the main foyer and its current place over the doorway leading into the room (not visible in any of the accompanying photographs). Truman didn't think it was right that people had been walking over the presidential seal all these years. His sense of history was too strong, however, to discard the seal altogether, even though it irked him that the eagle was facing the wrong way—toward the arrows of war. Truman issued an executive order to change the presidential coat of arms so that in future, the United States eagle would always turn toward the right, the direction of honor, and face the olive branch of peace. On the television tour, Truman also mentioned how much he enjoyed the fact that when he exited the White House from the Diplomatic Reception Room, he looked toward the Washington Monument and Jefferson Memorial.

According to the literary former first dog Millie, two of her pups, after running around the White House in the wet grass, stopped in the China Room to dry their feet. To their amazement, they discovered a magnificent white collie. The dog that captured their attention was the long-since-deceased Rob Roy, the Coolidge's stately canine, featured prominently in the Howard Chandler Christy painting of Grace Coolidge that hangs on the south wall of the China Room. Rob Roy was the president's favorite dog, the first lady preferring Prudence Prim. (The Coolidge's love of animals was so widely known that, during their tenure at the White House, dogs, cats, birds, a raccoon, a baby bear, a wallaby, a pair of lion cubs, an antelope, a large white goose, a donkey, a pygmy hippo, and a bobcat were presented to them as presents. Calvin Coolidge would take the raccoon on a leash for walks around the grounds of the White House and his wife would let her birds fly free in the executive mansion.)

Although the Christy painting is not visible in the photograph above, its impact is nevertheless felt. The red color scheme of the room has been traditionally determined by Mrs. Coolidge's red dress. Christy was supposed to paint Calvin Coolidge on the day he came to the White House in 1924, but the president was too preoccupied with the Teapot Dome Scandal to sit for him. The first lady posed instead.

Every first lady has her portrait painted and hung in the White House after she leaves. Those of Nancy Reagan, Rosalynn Carter, Betty Ford, and Patricia Nixon hang in the ground-floor corridor, just outside the doorway seen in the photograph above.

China Room

Not every first family needed to order a set of state china, not as long as a table could be laid for up to 102 guests with dishes from previous administrations. But when enough dishes had broken to make the number fall below the prerequisite, the first lady, for it was nearly always she, had an opportunity to go shopping, show off her personal taste in tableware, and order 120 place settings for the president's house. The China Room, displaying china used in every administration since George Washington's, shows how styles have changed. What never changes is the need to eat and drink, and for the president and first lady to be able to entertain in a manner fitting the Office of President of the United States.

The history of official White House china also reflects aspects of America's growth as an industrial nation. Until Lenox made a set of china for President Woodrow Wilson in 1913, all dishes used for state functions were made of fine French and English porcelain. There was no American firm that could produce the quality in the quantity the White House required. As late as 1902, a leading manufacturer of porcelain in Ohio turned down an order worth $50,000 from President Theodore Roosevelt, stating that it was too large; their entire business would be disrupted if they accepted. The order eventually went to Wedgewood in England.

First families frustrated at being unable to purchase American-made china still could request native designs, and there were ways to project patriotism onto the porcelain-perfect surfaces. Monroe's dinner plate carried the arms of the United States in the center, with a border of vignettes representing strength, agriculture, commerce, art, and science.

No dinner service was stranger than the famous Rutherford B. Hayes set, commissioned in 1879. Made by Haviland in France but designed by *Harper's Weekly* artist Theodore Davis, the set included plates fashioned after snowshoes; platters with shad swimming and turkeys strutting at sunrise; smaller plates featuring an Indian at a campfire alongside a dead deer, bison bracing in a blizzard, and big horns against the open sky; plates with okra, mayflowers, and locust blossoms; and dozens of weirdly shaped pieces of Limoges showing Native American species of bird, fish, flower, and mammal. The wife of the senator from Maine, Mrs. James G. Blaine, wrote: "It is worth a trip from New York to Washington to see the table at a State Dinner at the White House."

In the twentieth century, almost every new state service incorporated at least a version of the presidential seal. Mrs. Lyndon Johnson continued the tradition of using American motifs on state dishes and chose as her inspiration wildflowers. She, like Mrs. Reagan after her, ordered 220 place settings.

Lady Bird Johnson's china was paid for by an anonymous donor. Nancy Reagan's red and gold banded china, ordered in 1981 and costing $209,508 for 4,372 pieces, was also paid for with private funds. Nevertheless, in this case there was a public outcry because it was a time of budget restraints. The arguments against Mrs. Reagan's buying the new dishes were the same as those waged against Martin Van Buren in the 1830s. After Van Buren was attacked for living too royally and possessing too many "cups and saucers," a defender replied: "They are wanted for a purpose which he [Van Buren's attacker] could never conjecture—the hospitable entertainment of visitors and friends—. They were used for the refreshment of the nation's guests."[4]

Vermeil Room

Located on the ground floor, the Vermeil Room was used for storage in the days of Madison and Jackson, Polk and Buchanan, Grant and McKinley. Then Theodore Roosevelt put it to use as a meeting room, and it remained as such until an affluent and munificent lady decided to bequeath the White House an exceedingly valuable collection. Margaret Thompson Biddle, an American heiress who had lived in Paris, accumulated an extensive array of vermeil and willed the 1,574 pieces to the White House when she died in 1956.

Vermeil, silver pieces that are dipped in gold, was popular in 1817 when President Monroe was refurnishing the White House, newly rebuilt after having been burned by the British in the War of 1812. Monroe showed his fondness for gilt by ordering a full service of vermeil flatware for the "President's Palace." (That was the name Pierre L'Enfant and the commissioners of the federal city called the executive mansion in the late eighteenth century. The press called it the "President's House." The people have always called it the "White House," and Theodore Roosevelt made that name official in 1901.)

The Eisenhowers exhibited the Biddle vermeil in 1958. This comprehensive collection contains pieces ranging from the Renaissance to the 1950s and includes the work of English Regency silversmith Paul Storr (1771–1844) and French Empire silversmith Jean-Baptiste-Claude Odiot (1763–1850). Individual pieces of vermeil are on display throughout the White House, and Biddle serving pieces and platters are used on state occasions. The tables for state dinners are still laid with gilt flatware; now, however, they are reproductions of an early-nineteenth-century design.

Both the miniature White House and the real White House excel in floral arrangements. After visiting both houses, the vision of the flowers remains.

If citizens find it somewhat unpalatable to see so much gold around the first house of democracy, it should be noted that not every goblet wetted the lips of a lord or financier. There is on display a footed cup engraved "The Agricultural Society of the Hundred of West Derby, to Ann Cockshead, of Lydiate, for raising a crop of potatoes, 1802," marked by Robert, David, and Samuel Hennell.

Every night, after the last White House guest has departed, the large floral arrangements filling each room with fragrance and beauty are refrigerated. In the morning, the dead flowers are discarded and replaced with fresh ones. In the replica, the magnificent mini-bouquets were originally made of bread dough and wilted only after about a decade, though mice nibbling the petals or rough handling accelerated their demise. Created by gardener Barbara Meyers of Chicago, the miniature arrangements, now made of a compound called Sculpey, are reductions of floral centerpieces that had at one time graced tables in the president's house.

Particularly noteworthy in this room is the French marble mantel dating from about 1825. A gift from the Museum of the City of New York, it was installed in 1962. It features two classically draped female figures on stiles facing a frieze of musicians.

A president has a singular relationship with the past and with the future, and living in the White House fortifies this connection. The chief executive shoulders the responsibility to uphold and protect the Constitution and the ideals of the founding fathers, to make daily decisions that show wisdom and vision, and to nourish a society and political system that will assure that worthy men and women will assume the challenge of leadership after he or she has left office.

George Washington surveyed the site of the White House, helped design the house, and drove in the first stakes, but he never lived there himself. John Adams was the first president to do so,

and no president could have provided a finer blessing than Adams did on the very first full day of his occupancy. To his wife he wrote on November 2, 1800: "I pray Heaven to bestow the best of blessings on this house, and on all that shall hereafter inhabit it. May none but honest and wise men ever rule under this roof!" Franklin Delano Roosevelt loved the benediction and had it carved into the mantel of the State Dining Room. It is fitting that the 1869 portrait by George P.A. Healy of Abraham Lincoln hangs above. Lincoln is contemplative, waiting, as the art historian William Kloss observes, to take action that "will be proper."

State Dining Room

Thomas Jefferson's office incorporated the space now known as the State Dining Room. "The room," writes William Seale of the third president, "was the center of his life."

In the light from its tall windows he wrote his letters and studied his maps. On freezing winter days he labored between two brimming log fires, abjuring in this private place the costly coal he had introduced elsewhere in the house. In the summertime, with the windows open, he might have been in a treehouse, so lofty and green were his views, and so remote was this corner room from other human activity.[5]

It was here that Jefferson wrote all his own official letters without the aid of a secretary, kept his gardening tools and potted plants, let his tamed mockingbird fly free, and readied his personal aide Meriwether Lewis for the expedition he was soon to embark on with William Clark.

With the coming of the Madisons in 1809—and Dolley's presence in the White House is remembered perhaps even more vividly than James'—Jefferson's office became the State Dining Room. The room was decorated with portraits of Washington, Adams, and Jefferson and little else. It was to this room, with forty places set for lunch, that Dolley Madison flew in August 1814 and ordered the painting of George Washington taken off the wall and saved from the advancing British troops.

Not as dramatic as Dolley Madison's escape during the War of 1812, but significant in American history, was Booker T. Washington's dining at the White House with President and Mrs. Theodore Roosevelt in 1901, the first African American to receive a social

The two side tables of mahogany and marble in the English Regency manner were designed by Stanford White for the renovation of the White House that took place under Theodore Roosevelt in 1902 and were modeled on a table in White's own home. The carved wood eagle pedestals were painted and gilded in 1961. The "fruit basket" (on the left with flowers) represents one of the bronze-doré treasures purchased by Monroe in 1817. The candelabrum is modeled after one from the Biddle vermeil collection.

The wineglass is similar to the simple glassware that has been used in the White House since the early 1960s. Jacqueline Kennedy ended a White House tradition of engraved stemware when she placed an order with the Morgantown Glass Guild in West Virginia. She was adamant in wanting to give jobs to Americans in what was an economically depressed area. When the manufacturer started to advertise "President's House Crystal" at $10 a dozen, Mrs. Kennedy said she did not mind at all.

Should you ever attend a state dinner, before you on the table will be a service plate; napkin; place card; menu card; three knives (fish, dinner, salad); three forks (fish, dinner, salad); and four glasses (water, white wine, red wine, champagne). During the course of the meal, you will also be presented with a dinner plate, salad plate, dessert plate, finger bowl, cup and saucer, dessert fork, dessert spoon and demitasse spoon. You will not be asked to help with the washing up.

The State Dining Room is set up for eighty guests. Round tables have been the preferred seating arrangement during recent administrations. The tiny gold chairs in the photographs are made in a metal mold. Each chair, made of light pewter, is 2 1/2 inches high and weighs 3 ounces.

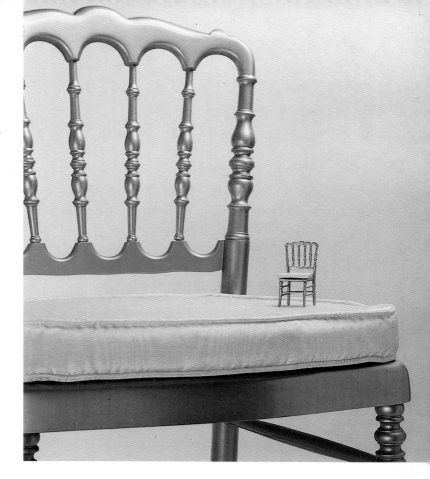

The horseshoe table was popular for state dinners until the early 1960s. About 96 people can be seated, up to 102 in a squeeze, but one can only converse with a small number.

The painted walls of the State Dining Room may not look distinguished at first glance, but they are actually hand-carved oak panels with Corinthian pilasters and a delicate frieze. Installed in 1902, they were painstakingly removed during the Truman renovation of 1948–52. The State Dining Room was the only room where, in 1952, all the original panels were put back in place. But as many were chipped or split, it was decided to paint the admirable old oak light green. Then, in 1961, it was painted bone white; in 1972 and 1981, antique white; and in 1985, off-white with an umber glaze.

invitation from the president of the United States. Groups not only in the South but also in the North railed against the gesture. Roosevelt reacted to the ranting by declaring he should have invited Washington sooner.

The State Dining Room has witnessed countless other historic events; and every time a president toasts a foreign dignitary, he tries, through the formality of a state dinner and familiarity of "breaking bread," to secure better and more peaceful relations. Most memorable in recent times was the Reagan state dinner for the Gorbachevs in 1987, marking the beginning of the end of the Cold War. On this occasion, Van Cliburn, who had become the first American to win the Tchaikovsky competition in Moscow during the days of heated East-West relations in the 1950s, played the piano after dinner.

Red Room

The red of the Red Room is all encompassing. Color, rather than history, makes the first impression. It is a favorite room of first ladies and guests alike, often used as a sitting room and for small teas and receptions. One likes to linger in the Blue Room because of historic associations. One loves to remain in the Red Room because it is so aesthetically satisfying.

During the presidency of Thomas Jefferson (1801–9), the Red Room was known as the "President's Antechamber," the room adjoining his office and set aside for those with appointments with the president. By the time of John Quincy Adams, the president's office was on the second floor and a pianoforte was ensconced in the Red Room. For most of the nineteenth century, this room was known as the "Music Room." The music stand to the right of the fireplace recalls this period.

When Lincoln was president, male guests retired to the Red Room for brandy and cigars after dinner.

The mantel is one of a pair purchased by President Monroe in 1818 from British agents in Italy. They were originally placed in the State Dining Room but were moved to the Red Room and Green Room during the Theodore Roosevelt renovation in 1902.

In the foreground is the sofa table with a fitted writing drawer and gilt winged sphinx support, attributed to the famous cabinetmaker Charles Lannuier. Over the mantel hangs one of the favorite paintings in the White House, the portrait of Martin Van Buren's daughter-in-law and official hostess, Angelica Singleton Van Buren, painted by Henry Inman in 1842. And above the doorway to the State Dining Room is a portrait of a man whose name is as well-known as most presidents'—John James Audubon. The portrait was painted in Scotland in 1826 when Audubon was finally, after great difficulty, having his bird drawings engraved. Although most people admire the John Syme portrait of the great naturalist, Audubon thought that the eyes there were "more those of an enraged Eagle than mine."

On the back wall, top right, is the 1804 portrait of Dolley Madison by Gilbert Stuart. The furniture in the room, all American Empire (1810–30) appears peculiar but thoroughly engaging to the contemporary eye. The sofa on the right is described by the White House Historical Society as "a remarkably beautiful Empire sofa with bronze sphinx heads under the arm supports, perhaps the finest such American piece known today." Guests to the White House still use it, as they do all the furniture in all the state rooms.

The gueridon (circular table) in front of the sofa is quite possibly the most finely crafted piece of furniture in the White House. Made by the Frenchman Charles Lannuier in 1815 in New York, this mahogany table supports a trompe l'oeil pattern of geometric pieces of fine-grained marbles inlaid on top. The table is stunning, and although it is on display and seen by over a million and a half visitors each year, only those fortunate enough to stand next to it appreciate just how lovely it is.

Here, in the parlor, he was known to put social form aside and ask his guests their opinions on the most pressing matters of the day. President Grant prohibited political talk in the Red Room. Every weeknight from 9:00 P.M. on, friends joined President and Mrs. Grant in the Red Room for drinks, cigars, chat, and parlor games. Although Washington can never be apolitical, the intent of these gatherings was to be purely social.

The Blue Room has the honor of having seen a president married. The Red Room is the only room in the White House that has witnessed a president sworn in. President Grant, fearing national disturbances because of the "fraudulent election" between Samuel Tilden and Rutherford B. Hayes, insisted that a smooth and unimpeded succession of authority take place. Because March 4, 1877, fell on a Sunday and the inauguration would therefore have to be postponed until the Monday, Grant arranged to have Hayes secretly sworn in in the Red Room on Sunday, unbeknownst to the thirty-eight dinner guests also in the house at the time.

The second Mrs. Wilson used the Red Room for teas during World War I, placating the ladies who left their cards at the north entrance and fulfilling her obligation to entertain the wives of important visitors to Washington.

Eleanor Roosevelt also met with women in the Red Room, but often for a different purpose. "To general astonishment," writes William Seale,

Mrs. Roosevelt announced early on that she too would hold press conferences . . . her initial one as First Lady took place in the Red Room on the Monday after her husband took office. Mrs. Roosevelt decided to give conferences as a special favor to women reporters, who were not admitted to the presidential press conferences. During the hard times of the

Depression years, inability to get good stories could cost them their jobs. "I shall never forget my first press conference," Mrs. Roosevelt wrote. "I could feel the disapproval of the ushers as I went in fear and trembling, trying to cover my uncertainty by passing around a large box of candy to fill in the first awkward moments."[6]

The Empire style, named after the first French Empire, was the last of the great classical styles of furniture. It reached its height at the time of Napoleon, 1804–14, and stayed in fashion until around 1825–30. The "look" was created largely by Napoleon's two young architects, Pierre François Leonard Fontaine and Charles Percier, both of whom had studied in Rome and were devoted to Greek and Roman ideals. They held French art under the Bourbon monarchs in contempt and believed that no one could surpass the ancients in forms of beauty. Two rooms in the White House, the Red and Blue, are decorated, as they were in the time of Monroe, in the Empire style.

After Napoleon's successful North African campaign, cabinetmakers working in the Empire style borrowed Egyptian motifs as well as Greek and Roman. Winged classical figures in flowing gowns, mythological and allegorical subjects, the imperial eagle, sphinxes, animals, fanciful monsters such as swans, griffins, and dolphins, and the paws of lions were all incorporated into furniture design. There was also a prevalence of Roman chariots, winged trumpets, Neptune's trident, swords, lances, and lyres.

The boldly curved sofa is an outstanding example of American Empire design. Perfectly symmetrical as all Empire furniture is, the sofa features carved dolphin legs with gilded heads and painted scaled bodies. Behind the sofa on the north wall are two mahogany card tables (c. 1815) with swan's head lyre pedestals. The side chairs date from the same period and are adaptions of classical Greek klismos form—a continuous curving line of frame and legs. The miniature sofa, including pillows, is carved wood with paint simulating fabric.

Blue Room

George Washington liked oval rooms. True, they were fashionable in the 1790s, but Washington also saw them as functional spaces for presidential levees, where he and his entourage could stand in a formal circle receiving callers. The Oval Office in the West Wing was inspired by the Blue Room and its sister room, the Yellow Oval, directly above. Although Washington did not live in the White House, he was one of the jurors in the 1792 competition to choose the designer of the executive mansion. James Hoban, the winner, was the only architect to have a private meeting with Washington before submitting plans, and the only one to include oval rooms as a central feature of the presidential mansion.

Thomas Jefferson would stand in the exact center of today's Blue Room to shake hands with visitors (Truman did the same). Neither Washington nor Adams felt it was appropriate to shake hands, making Jefferson, the author of the Declaration of Independence, the first president to reach out physically to his constituents. President Lincoln stood just inside the Blue Room door, and sometimes the crowds wanting to shake *his* hand were so long they extended out the north entrance and down the street. Lincoln's hand suffered sorely, but still he continued the practice, always believing the people should have access to their president. On January 1, 1865, African Americans, whose forebears had served as slaves in the Jefferson, Madison, Jackson, Polk, and Taylor White Houses (all Southern presidents), joined the line to the Blue Room to meet *and* shake the hand of the author of the Emancipation Proclamation.

Many presidents and first ladies have received guests in the Blue Room, the unparalleled and preemi-

Anyone attending a White House reception may sit on the most famous furniture in the house. The Bellangé chairs and sofa are celebrated not only because President Monroe ordered them from France in 1817, determined to acquire for the president's house even finer furniture than the British had burned three years previously, but also because the chairs and sofa were sold in auction by James Buchanan in 1860 and Jacqueline Kennedy went on a treasure hunt one hundred years later to get them back. Mrs. Kennedy concurred with President Monroe, who had stated that the cost of furnishing the White House was high because the furniture was "not less deserving attention than the building for which it is intended."

The gilt beechwood furniture was supposed to be mahogany, as James Monroe had requested, but the purchasing agents in France thought that mahogany was not suitable for a gentleman's home, and certainly not for a head of state. Some historians now suggest that the true reason may have been a shortage of the wood. The French Empire—sometimes described as ancient Roman—chairs and sofa were part of an original order that included eighteen armchairs, eighteen side chairs, two sofas, two bergères (large armchairs with upholstered sides, to be used by the president and first lady), four stools, six footstools, two screens, and one pier table. Except for the pier table, everything was auctioned in 1860 and replaced with Victorian furniture.

Monroe was able to buy other French pieces at bargain prices. He had specified that he wanted items with eagles (even though the Blue Room furniture, specially made, had none). In France, all those imperial eagles that had been fashionable with Napoleon were now passé under the reign of Louis XVIII. The warehouses were full of orphaned eagles looking for a republican home.

In the first three photographs, the Diplomatic Reception Room carpet was substituted for the unfinished Blue Room rug (see page 187).

nent reception room in the house. Only one, however, was married there (although another, Rutherford B. Hayes, chose this room in which to renew his marriage vows on his twenty-fifth wedding anniversary). On June 2, 1886, during the first term of Grover Cleveland's interrupted presidency (Benjamin Harrison was president between the two terms), he wed the young Frances Folsom and provided the press with the love story of the decade.

The Blue Room has hosted many guests and diverse groups. Mrs. Benjamin Harrison allowed the founders of the Daughters of the American Revolution to meet in the Blue Room, thereby giving them not only a needed space, but also a high profile and lobbying power in the days when women still did not have the vote. FDR set up barrels of beer outside the Blue Room door for the press on the first day they came to the White House after the lifting of prohibition.

The furniture that Monroe had purchased for the Blue Room was more than forty years old when bachelor James Buchanan and Harriet Lane, his niece and official hostess, decided that a change was in order. They wanted what William Seale calls "rather clumsy furniture in the Louis XV revival style . . . carved, fully gilded, and upholstered in blue brocatelle." Before they made their purchases, however, they decided in 1860 to auction fifty items of White House furniture. It is almost certain that the Empire Blue Room suite was part of the sale.

In 1961, Jacqueline Kennedy found the only remaining piece of furniture from Monroe's 1817 purchase, a table, in the basement of the White House. It took six weeks to restore its former splendor. The table was featured in a newspaper article that was seen by Catherine Bohlen of Villanova, Pennsylvania, who recognized it as matching a Bellangé chair in her possession. She presented the armchair to the White House, and then Mrs. Kennedy proceeded to have reproductions of it made by American craftsmen. Her idea was to decorate the Blue Room in the period of the Monroe presidency. As more original chairs and eventually the sofa were located and acquired by the White House, the reproductions were removed and replaced with originals. There are now five original chairs in the room, each with an identifying plaque on the back. And one added note: from Buchanan's purchase of furniture, only the large "circular divan or ottoman sofa" remains in the White House today, and it has been relegated to storage.

The Bellangé sofa fits perfectly the contour of the room. The wallpaper is a reproduction of a fragment of a French Directoire paper of about 1800. The painting on the wall, one of the most intriguing and expertly executed paintings in the White House, is of the tenth president, John Tyler, and is by the same artist, George P. A. Healy, who did the Lincoln portrait in the State Dining Room. As well as masterfully portraying Tyler's character, Healy included documents referring to the major accomplishments of his administration. But the surprising feature is the rumpled newspaper in the president's hand. We learn from the art historian William Kloss that the *National Intelligencer*, which was supposed to be an impartial recorder of government affairs (the precursor to the *Congressional Record*), had come out in favor of Henry Clay's anti-Tyler policies. About the *Intelligencer*, Tyler is reported to have said: "I can no longer tolerate the Intelligencer, as the official paper . . . There is a point beyond which one's patience cannot endure."[7] Healy has caught Tyler at the moment of crumpling the newspaper, readying it, we suppose, for the flames.

Green Room

The second American revolution took place at Thomas Jefferson's dinner parties. Protocol, Jefferson believed, was courtly and in opposition to republican values. He affronted the wife of the British ambassador (who called himself Envoy Extraordinary and Minister Plenipotentiary for His Britannic Majesty) by not taking her arm and accompanying her to the table. After she created a stir in the diplomatic corps, Jefferson remarked, "I blush to have to put so much trash on paper," and then issued the following statement to his cabinet: "When brought together in society all are perfectly equal, whether foreign or domestic, titled or untitled, in or out of office,"[8] underscoring the point that title and grade of diplomat gave no preference in the New World. European diplomats were appalled that the American president was known to pay more attention on occasion to "aborigines from the West" than to ambassadors.

The White House replica creates an illusion of authenticity because absolutely everything is in scale. The chairs are perfectly proportioned even though they are less than 3 inches tall, and tiny electrical cords lead from miniature lamps whose light bulbs burn at different intensities. Nothing is omitted, not even the light switch, seen on the north wall. The walls of the Green Room in the real White House are covered in moss green moiré silk. But moiré doesn't come in scale. If the Zweifels had covered the walls of the miniature with the same moiré silk used in the White House, the scale would be wrong and the *illusion* lost. Instead, using a variety of paints and brushes, the Zweifels carefully miniaturized their "moiré silk" on an oil cloth, which was then applied to the walls of the replica.

The playing cards and checkers are used for scale. During the Monroe administration, the Green Room was a card room with whist the game of choice. Macaroni, waffles, and even ice cream were also considered as props for the scale photograph. All three foods were introduced into America by Thomas Jefferson and may well have been served first in this room.

This second revolution was fought, in part, in the Green Room, Jefferson's common dining room. The president did not draw up seating charts worked out by rank; guests had to choose their own seats at the "democratic" round or oval table. Serving the best imported wines with delectable French cuisine helped mollify most imperious guests. One could be guaranteed fascinating conversation and wonderful food at the Jefferson White House, but not conventional dining.

Traditionally, there would be a servant to attend every one or two guests at a meal. This buzz of activity was eliminated by Jefferson. Instead, he used dumbwaiters, which were really small tables with compartments from which food could be served and on which dirty dishes could be placed. The host had responsibility for the largest of these dumbwaiters, and others were placed around the table. Only the host ever had to rise from his place during the meal. Servants did bring in the dishes that needed to be very hot, but they quickly departed. The food was served by the host and his "deputies" at the table and dishes were passed around. A guest could speak on any subject, no matter how delicate, without worry that she would be overheard by a servant who had received a "gratuity" from a journalist who craved confidential information. Jefferson also devised a rather intriguing system of pulleys to bring food up from the kitchen and turnstile-type trays built into the walls on which food was conveyed in and out of the dining room.

The Green Room was James Madison's office, and it is thought that in June 1812, he signed the declaration of war against Great Britain here. By John Quincy Adams' presidency, the room had become the

The first deliberate effort to decorate any room in the White House in a historic style did not occur until late in the 1920s under the Coolidges. It took time for furniture to transform itself from old to antique and for the occupants of the White House to see that there was more inherent interest in having rooms recall the past than be exemplars of modern taste.

The Green Room has always seemed to be the guinea pig, sacrificed by first ladies to expert advisory committees whose mission it was to help decorate individual White House rooms. Grace Coolidge's committee was essentially the same group of people who oversaw the installation of the new American Wing at the Metropolitan Museum of Art. Jacqueline Kennedy's Fine Arts Committee of the White House was headed by Henry Francis du Pont, founder of the Winterthur Museum of Decorative Arts. Both committees decided the Green Room should be decorated in the Federal style.

The furniture in the Green Room today dates from the period of 1780 to 1820. Pat Nixon, advised by Clement Conger, a former White House curator, and Edward Vason Jones, a designer who had helped organize the Metropolitan Museum of Art's 1970 exhibition of nineteenth-century decorative arts, secured many of the fine examples of Federal furniture for the White House collection. The pier tables along the far (north) wall and the side chairs next to them, the worktables alongside the fireplace, the easy chair on the right of the fireplace, and the sofa are all attributed to the New York workshop of Duncan Phyfe.

Perhaps because silver improves with age, but also because of its simple, elegant lines, the Sheffield coffee urn on the sofa table captivates the eye. If one comes close enough, the monogram "JAA" (John and Abigail Adams) can be discerned. Flanking it are a pair of candlesticks purchased by James Monroe in Paris around 1789 and sold to his good friend James Madison in 1803. Monroe needed to raise cash to help defray personal expenses when he returned to Paris to negotiate the Louisiana Purchase.

The portrait of John Quincy Adams by Gilbert Stuart is on the back wall, top left. His wife, Louisa, graces the same spot on the right-hand side of the doorway. Hers is the more revealing portrait, a character study for all ages.

The painting below that of John Quincy Adams is one of the most intriguing in the White House collection and not in keeping either thematically or stylistically with other works. Titled *The Mosquito Net*, it was painted by John Singer Sargent in 1912 and shows one of his sister's friends asleep underneath what Sargent called the *garde-mangers*, or "protection from the eaters." Perhaps the symbolic quality of protection from bloodsucking pests appeals to politicians and accounts for the painting's prominent place in the White House.

"Green Drawing Room" because of the color of the draperies and upholsteries. Green had been the color of the floor covering earlier, too.

The Green Room has been associated with many gracious presidential entertainments. It was Monroe's "Card Room" and Mrs. Theodore Roosevelt's receiving room for guests attending the weekly Friday musicales and concerts in the East Room. Crowds of people at large gala receptions have overflowed into this room, where countless cups of tea have been poured and hands shaken. Mrs. Bush entertained visiting dignitaries here.

Two of the saddest events in White House history have Green Room associations, and both involve children of presidents. Willie Lincoln, who died of typhoid fever at age eleven, was embalmed in the Green Room. His grief-stricken parents remained upstairs in the opposite corner of the house until the day of the funeral. Abraham, Mary, and Robert Lincoln then came down to the Green Room, locked the door, and mourned their young son and brother until it was time for the service to begin.

One hundred and one years later, two small children stood with their nanny at the door of the Green Room. They looked into the East Room, where a coffin had been placed, and heard mass for their father, John F. Kennedy.

The Benjamin Franklin portrait (sometimes called the "thumb portrait") sits above the mantel like a favorite aged uncle in a great-aunt's parlor. The man is approachable, warm and beneficent even if the surroundings are not. It is a wonderful painting of the most famous American of his day, made in 1767 by David Martin, a Scotsman. According to legend, two young men had a property dispute and agreed to let Benjamin Franklin settle it. The man who won the quarrel commissioned the portrait, and the papers Franklin holds are not government documents but the disputed property deeds. Martin painted Franklin as sympathetic and sagacious, a model of wisdom and common sense.

Franklin D. Roosevelt approved the design for the piano, hardly everyone's idea of elegant styling, and Steinway presented it to the White House in 1938. Truman thought it had one of the most wonderful tones of any piano he had ever heard. On the television tour he conducted through the renovated White House, he seemed to get most enjoyment from sitting at the piano and playing for the huge home audience watching him on their newly purchased 1950s TV sets.

Hundreds of musicians, dancers, and vocalists have performed in the East Room, the nation's oldest showcase for the performing arts. On January 1, 1801, the Marine Band, the oldest performing arts company in the country, gave its first concert. (John Philip Sousa was its leader between 1880 and 1892.) John Tyler, whose daughter-in-law was an actress before her marriage, was the first president to invite performing artists to the White House.

Some of the artists and groups who have performed in the East Room are Kate Smith, Marian Anderson, Artur Rubinstein, Gregor Piatigorsky, Leonard Bernstein, Roberta Peters, Pablo Casals, Jerome Robbins, Isaac Stern, American Ballet Theater, Robert Joffrey Ballet, Robert Merrill, New Christy Minstrels, Dave Brubeck Quartet, Maria Tallchief, Shirley Jones, Leontyne Price, Richard Tucker, Rudolf Serkin, José Limon, Tony Bennett, Van Cliburn, Robert Goulet, Martha Graham Dance Company, Modern Jazz Quartet, Peggy Lee, Pearl Bailey, André Watts, Anna Moffo, Frank Sinatra, Beverly Sills, Ann-Margret, Benny Goodman, Itzhak Perlman, Perry Como, Eugenia and Pinchas Zukerman, Sherrill Milnes, Mstislav Rostropovich, Jessye Norman, Johnny Mathis, Marilyn Horne, Lionel Hampton, Harry Connick Jr., and Frederica von Stade.

East Room

The White House is the people's house, and no room is more symbolic of the right of public access than the East Room. Since the days of Jefferson, the public has been able to enter the house, at times with hardly any restrictions, at other times with entry only permitted to the East Room. Every president who has lived in the White House has understood that he was the tenant, the American people the landlords. Except at times of national emergency, the public could call at the White House and imagine that one day, someone in their family might be president and live at 1600 Pennsylvania Avenue.

A "democratic" levee during the time of Andrew Jackson was described by English journalist and social reformer Harriet Martineau as follows:

One of the most remarkable sights in the country is the President's levee . . . Men go there in plaid cloaks and leather belts, with all manner of wigs, and offer a large variety of obeisance to the chief magistrate [President]. Women go in bonnets and shawls, talk about the company, stand upon chairs to look over people's heads and stare at the large room . . . To see such people mixed in with foreign ambassadors and their suites, to observe the small mutual knowledge of classes and persons who thus meet on terms of equality, is amusing enough . . . If the gentry of Washington desire to do away with the custom, they must be unaware of the dignity which resides in it and which is apparent to the eyes of a stranger . . . Some looked merry; some looked busy, but none bashful.[9]

It was not until 1829, during Jackson's administration that the populace and dignitaries actually had something worthy to look at in the East Room, be-sides each other. Prior to this time, the large reception room had not been furnished, no congressional appropriation being forthcoming. Jefferson divided the room into office spaces, with Meriwether Lewis of Lewis and Clark fame occupying one compartment at the south end. Madison used this space for his cabinet meetings. Later, a live alligator belonging to Lafayette was kept here. During the Civil War, Union troops were billeted in this room, the largest in the house. Indeed, because for most of its two-hundred-year history the East Room has been essentially a big (2,844 square feet), nearly empty space, it has been the most versatile room in the White House.

Japanese lacquered boxes, porcelain vases, silks, foodstuffs, and objects made of paper and straw, brought back from the Far East by Commodore Matthew Perry and never before seen in the United States, were displayed in the East Room by President Franklin Pierce in 1857 for the public's benefit. Japanese wrestlers, another oriental curiosity, were entreated to show their skill against their American counterparts in a match instigated and refereed by President Theodore Roosevelt. The use of the East Room as gymnasium continued when Roosevelt invited Chinese wrestlers to perform in front of about sixty guests, including senators and cabinet members. "Mr. Roosevelt expressed offhandedly," recalled White House chief usher "Ike" Hoover, who came to the White House as an electrician in 1891 and remained forty-two years, "a wish to take on one of the big fellows."[10]

A versatile man, Teddy Roosevelt also believed rooms should be multipurpose, and the East Room hosted many different types of performances during his administration. It was during his years as president that the East Room became the focal point for the performing arts. As White House music historian Elise Kirk notes, many musical firsts occurred during Teddy's reign. Among these were the first full concert by a noted pianist (Ignacy Jan Paderewski, who would play for five other presidents); the first musicale devoted to a single opera; the installation of the first East Room piano, an extremely ornate but fine concert grand from Steinway and Sons; and the first performance of Scott Joplin's "Maple Leaf Rag" (at the instigation of Teddy's daughter Alice). On January 15, 1904, a twenty-eight-year-old cellist named Pablo Casals performed in the East Room and later said of his host, "I felt that in a sense [Roosevelt] personified the American nation, with all his energy, strength and confidence."[11] On November 13, 1961, Casals would play for another vigorous, young president, John F. Kennedy.

Woodrow Wilson invited the Senate Foreign Relations Committee to the East Room to discuss ratification of the Treaty of Versailles and the League of Nations. Wilson failed to win the approval he sought, but twenty-four years and another world war later, the East Room hosted forty-four representatives from the newly formed United Nations. Around a great table, the U.N. members signed an agreement to establish the United Nations Relief and Rehabilitation Administration, fulfilling one of Wilson's long-awaited dreams.

In this room where Lincoln had lain in state, President Lyndon Johnson signed the Civil Rights Act on July 2, 1964, thus expanding and extending the task the sixteenth president had so rightly begun. Perhaps it is this combination of taking the torch, the title, and living in the same house that gives the American presidency its vital resonance.

The East Room is identified with weddings, deaths, momentous news briefings, bill signings, and gala black and white tie evenings with dazzling and often brilliant entertainment. Elizabeth Tyler, Nellie Grant, Alice Roosevelt, and Lynda Bird Johnson were married here. Susan Ford's classmates held their senior prom in this room. The funerals of Presidents Harrison, Taylor, Lincoln, McKinley, Franklin Roosevelt, and Kennedy were held here.

One intent of the nineteenth-century levee was to give the people an opportunity to see the president in his home. With the advent of television, millions can now watch as the press question the chief executive, historic legislation and treaties are signed into law, and renowned artists perform in the East Room. The room has always been, and continues to be, the country's "audience room."

In a letter dated November 21, 1800, to her daughter Nabby, Abigail Adams, the first first lady to reside in the White House, wrote: "The house is made habitable, but there is not a single fence, yard or other convenience, without, and the great unfinished audience-room I make a drying-room of, to hang up the clothes in."

In 1930, Mrs. Herbert Hoover gave a linen shower for one of her secretaries soon to be married. It was held in the East Room, and to the surprise of the bride-to-be and the delight of historically informed guests, she hung the presents on a clothesline across the room. White House usher Ike Hoover commented, "It really looked like a typical washline, full of clothes on Monday morning. It was Monday, by the way."

The replica of the East Room piano measures 12 inches long, 3 1/2 inches high. The miniature chandeliers are 10 inches high.

The size (79 feet by 36 feet, with 19-foot 10-inch ceilings) of the East Room makes the first impression upon the visitor. Not large in comparison with the halls in the great houses and palaces of Europe, it was enormous by nineteenth-century American standards. The room was as large as Abraham Lincoln's entire house in Springfield. The Garfield boys, Irwin (age eleven) and Abram (age nine), rode their velocipedes and the Roosevelt children roller-skated in this great empty space.

The second powerful impression comes from the three chandeliers, immense by any standards. The north and south fixtures are each made up of 6,137 pieces of cut Bohemian glass; the central chandelier has 12 additional drops. The bottom crystal hangs only 9 feet 1 1/2 inches above the floor. It takes one man two days to clean one chandelier.

These massive lights were particularly difficult to miniaturize and electrify. John Zweifel had to find a glassblower who could blow the entire 10-inch-high chandelier in one piece, but with such delicate designs that it looked to be constructed of over 6,000 crystal drops. Each miniature chandelier has 55 light bulbs the size of a grain of rice and 110 hairlike electrical wires that need to be coaxed into tiny, tight openings by hands that in comparison look like giants' appendages.

The single object in the White House with the greatest aura is the Gilbert Stuart portrait of George Washington. It was not painted from life, and its exalted position comes not from artistic merit but from the fact that it is the only object that has continuously been in the house since the earliest days. The father of our country has watched over every president from John Adams to Bill Clinton. His presence is a moving tribute to constitutional government and the peaceful succession of leadership as symbolized by the flow of first families through the White House. The folios at Washington's feet are the Constitution and Laws of the United States. Washington, in his civilian clothes, reaches out to the unknown, but reaches out with an open hand and a courageous heart nevertheless. If a painting can be a conscience, this is it. Each president has felt that his administration marks a new beginning, but Washington's marked the initiation of a new nation. Under him, America was born.

Dolley Madison saved the George Washington portrait for posterity. Just minutes before the British entered the White House on August 24, 1814, determined to burn it to the ground, Dolley Madison had the frame broken and the picture removed from the wall. The new furniture could go up in flames, but not George Washington, the father of the country. The young nation needed the few symbols it had, and Washington was one of the most beloved.

Martha Washington, on the left, never leaves her husband's side. The portrait, painted in 1878 by Eliphalet Andrews, lacks fidelity. The head, supposedly modeled after a Gilbert Stuart portrait, is perhaps most accurate; but the body is a pastiche, and the dress is by Worth, a Parisian couturier active a century after Martha Washington's time.

On the right of George Washington is the John Singer Sargent portrait of Theodore Roosevelt. It is a masterful painting and some argue, the best presidential portrait in the house. Roosevelt himself liked it "enormously." On artistic merit alone, it deserves its prominent place. But perhaps Roosevelt is honored in the East Room because it is due to him, and his architect Charles McKim, that the East Room looks the way it does today. The elegant painted wood paneled walls with the low-relief wood carvings, the marble mantels, the huge chandeliers, the Marie Antoinette pattern parquet floors—all these were introduced during the renovation that took place in 1902.

Main Stairway to Family Quarters

Down these stairs come the president and first lady on every state occasion held at the White House. Tall or short, imposing or not, no one can ignore the entrance of the chief executive when the Marine Band strikes up the first chords of "Hail to the Chief." This is the ceremonial staircase, and it is here that the president, first lady, and their guests of honor are photographed before proceeding to the East Room, where the other guests are gathered. The walk down the red carpet is surely the most romantic image of the presidency. Here is the pomp. Most of the rest of the time, the president is subject to circumstance.

First Lady's Dressing Room

A small, sunny room, the First Lady's Dressing Room has always been a private corner of a very public residence. So private, that in 1801 it was given one of the few water closets in the big, preplumbing house. President Franklin Pierce installed the first stationary bathtub in 1853. Prior to that, men only could bathe in a facility in the east pavilion, and women used portable sitz or hip tubs and shoe-shaped bathtubs made of tin. Dolley Madison bemoaned not being able to save her bathtub from the British in 1814. She was obligated to give precedence to government papers, the silver, and George Washington's portrait.

Located at the southwest corner of the house, this room adjoins the chamber that traditionally has been the master bedroom. Sometimes the presidents' children occupied the room, as did Tad Lincoln and Robert Johnson; sometimes the president reserved it for himself, as did Rutherford Hayes, who labeled it his sanctum or "den." But generally it was the first ladies who called it their own. Ida Saxon McKinley, an epileptic, spent many quiet hours sitting and knitting here; Lou Hoover put in a daybed for afternoon naps and a desk for keeping accounts and correspondence; and Nancy Reagan, who decorated it as in the photograph, used it as a dressing room.

The couple who seemed to take the greatest pleasure in this intimate space were President Woodrow and Mrs. Edith Bolling Wilson, the president's second wife. As newlyweds, they found privacy in this corner of the house. The room, since the addition of the bathroom and water closet, had an awkward shape with an off-centered fireplace. Nevertheless, Wilson dressed here, and he and his wife had breakfast, tea, and sometimes lunch or dinner in this crowded space.

With a fire burning, Andrew Johnson's magnificent magnolia tree almost tickling the panes of glass of the large south-facing window, and a perfect view of the Washington Monument, it is obvious why they found it such a pleasant place to be together.

Being pragmatic, Eleanor Roosevelt installed a single bed and slept here. She converted the spacious room next door into her sitting room to accommodate her many and frequent visitors. She and Franklin, whose bedroom was the next room over, had used separate rooms since 1918. Bess and Harry Truman occupied the same rooms as the Roosevelts, Mrs. Truman also choosing to use the dressing room as a bedroom and the larger room as her sitting room.

When the Reagans moved into the White House in January 1981, plans had already been laid to refurbish the second and third floors of the White House. They raised nearly a million dollars from friends and political supporters. Mrs. Reagan enlisted the help of a Los Angeles interior designer and old friend, Ted Graber, to help her make the living quarters "warm and livable." The master bedroom, never seen by the public but here displayed in the replica, beautifully fulfills Mrs. Reagan and Graber's objectives.

The Chinese paper, hand-painted in eighteenth-century style, gives the presidential bedroom its individuality. The lovely, delicate irregular spacing of a wide variety of birds—peacocks, bluebirds, roosters, etc.—around the room creates an airy, open field of color and form.

In order to replicate and reduce the wallpaper for the miniature White House, John and Jan Zweifel made a scale painting of the wallpaper onto a 10-by-12-inch sheet of paper. This was then carefully reduced on a color copier to provide sheets of paper for the walls of the miniature room.

The two diminutive chairs are only 3 inches high and 2 inches wide.

President and First Lady's Bedroom

After the swearing in, the parade, and the inaugural balls, the new president and first lady return to sleep in a room occupied only the previous night by another president and first lady. The changeover in the White House from one family to the next is so fast, so complete, one thinks that it must be done with a sorcerer's magic wand. The president and first lady's bedroom, the most private room in the house, humanizes the peaceful, incredible succession of power. To be able to call the White House home is the ultimate reward for those seeking to serve their country, and an honor bestowed on so few.

All the White House transitions have been swift (except the one from Lincoln to Johnson), but not always sweet. When President and Mrs. Pierce returned from the 1853 inaugural ball, there was no bedroom ready for them, which they considered a great indignity. Woodrow Wilson, who attended no ball but who celebrated first with his family and then at a smoker given for him by Princeton alumni at the Shoreham Hotel, found himself in the White House at midnight ringing assorted bells, not knowing which was which. Wearing only his underwear, he inquired if anyone had seen his trunk. He had no pajamas and, presumably, no toothbrush.

This room was Eleanor Roosevelt's and Bess Truman's sitting room/study but Jacqueline Kennedy reverted it to a bedroom as it had been for most of the nineteenth and early twentieth century. On inaugural night, though, the room was not yet ready, and she slept down the hall in the Queen's Bedroom. Eventually, it was decorated in shades of pale green and blue, and her furniture from her Georgetown house was moved in. The president's bedroom was across the hall, furnished with an eighteenth-century Chippendale high chest and a mahogany four-poster bed. Mrs. Kennedy did much of her work and her thinking in this bedroom suite.

It was in this room that Willie Lincoln died in the great "Lincoln" bed (see page 186) and James Garfield lay prostrate for months from an assassin's bullet. Because of Garfield's discomfort during the sweltering D.C. summer of 1881, doctors and engineers introduced the first air conditioning system in the United States to cool the dying president.

William McKinley was asleep here when an usher entered the room and whispered in his ear that the secretary of the navy was on the telephone with an important message. The battleship *Maine* had exploded and sunk in Havana harbor just hours before.

In this room, the first Mrs. Wilson passed away, and Woodrow Wilson suffered the stroke that would leave him an invalid for the rest of his life. For weeks he lay here helpless on the huge Lincoln bed.

On April 12, 1945, Eleanor Roosevelt was called to her sitting room and told of her husband's death at Warm Springs. She then summoned to her room the vice-president, who came directly from presiding over the Senate. Truman later wrote, "That was the first inkling I had of the seriousness of the situation." William Seale describes the exchange as follows: "Was there anything he could do for her? Eleanor Roosevelt replied, 'Is there anything *we* can do for *you?* For you are the one in trouble now.'"[12]

President's Study

Walls cannot talk, but if they could, the most dramatic stories these four would tell would center on the years 1933 to 1945. This was Franklin Delano Roosevelt's bedroom. An early riser, the invalid president would often conduct business from his bed. Francis Perkins, secretary of labor, described the bed and surrounding furniture as follows:

a small, narrow white iron bedstead, the kind one sees in the boy's room of many an American house. It had a thin, hard looking mattress, a couple of pillows, and an ordinary white seersucker spread. A folded old gray shawl lay at the foot . . . A white painted table, the kind one often sees in bathrooms, stood beside the bed, with a towel over it and with aspirin, nose drops, a glass of water, stubs of pencils, bits of paper with telephone numbers, addresses and memoranda to himself, a couple of books, a worn old prayer book, a watch, a package of cigarettes, an ash tray, a couple of telephones, all cluttered together.[13]

If the president was suffering from one of his chronic colds, the cabinet members would meet in this room. Aides would bring up memoranda and messages, and the papers of state would mingle with personal memorabilia. The mantel, seen on the left of the photograph, held miniature "Mexican pigs, Irish pigs, pigs of all kinds, sizes and colors" alongside family photographs, recalled Perkins.

FDR was an avid collector of many things, and one hobby in particular, stamp collecting, prepared him, quite unexpectedly, for his role as commander in chief during World War II. His naval aide during the war, Captain John L. McCrea, commented many years later that "the President's knowledge of world geography was amazing. I once expressed surprise that he knew so much about an insignificant lake in a small foreign country." "If a stamp collector really studies his stamps," replied FDR, "he can pick up a great deal of information." This geographical knowledge, often far exceeding that of others under his command, was vital during the war years.

The room appears as it did during the Reagan presidency. The red and white furniture came from Ronald and Nancy Reagan's California home. The desk lamp was made from a fire chief's silver horn, given to President Reagan when he was governor. The furnishings are cozy, comfortable, and familiar because it was here that the Reagans liked to relax. They looked forward to the evenings when dinner was served on trays in front of the television. Within these four walls, there was the semblance of a normal life.

Yellow Oval Room

In 1809, Dolley Madison chose yellow for the prevailing color in the upstairs Oval Room. In 1961, Jacqueline Kennedy decided the room should be decorated with antiques of the Louis XVI style of late-eighteenth-century France. The suite of furniture includes four side chairs and two armchairs made around 1800 by Jean-Baptiste Lelarge. A set of four carved and gilded armchairs were made by C. Sené, also of the Louis XVI period, two of which can be seen in the foreground. This neoclassical style was strongly influenced by Greek and Roman furnishings discovered during the excavations at Pompeii and Herculaneum in the late 1750s. The candelabra on the two French Louis XV commodes flanking the mantel were given by Princess Elizabeth of Great Britain in 1951 when she visited President and Mrs. Harry Truman.

Royalty and gold candelabra were not Harry's "style." He'd rather have watched a local baseball game and sit outdoors on a balmy summer's evening. Truman unilaterally decided that a balcony should be added to the second-floor Oval Room, against the loud protests of architects and historians. Truman got his balcony, with its good view of local playing fields, and he thoroughly enjoyed using it. If you want to know what his architectural transgression looks like, pull out a $20 bill.

When Millard and Abigail Fillmore moved into the White House in 1850 after the death of Zachary Taylor, there was not a Bible or dictionary or any other book to be found. Mrs. Fillmore, a former schoolteacher, did not consider a house a home without a library, and if this big white "temple of inconveniences," as her husband described it, was to be habitable for herself, her family, and future first families, there had to be books. They received money from Congress to buy some, and in the second-floor Oval Room she created her library and family room.

The Yellow Oval Room is one of the prettiest rooms in the house. Three stately windows facing the south lawn, Washington Monument, and Jefferson Memorial provide one of the best views in Washington and flood the room with light.

This room has always been central, literally and figuratively, in the lives of the occupants of the White House. For most of the two hundred years of the house's history, it was the boundary between the family's bedrooms and either the president's executive offices (in the nineteenth century) or the official guest rooms. Sometimes the Yellow Room was strictly a family room where children and parents would meet nightly to read, sing, play musical instruments, hang Christmas stockings, and relax, as during the administrations of Fillmore, Lincoln, Hayes, Theodore Roosevelt, and Wilson. The Hayeses sang psalms, and Wilson read the Bible aloud. Harding and his friends played poker and drank bootleg liquor.

Sometimes this room would serve as the president's private office, where he could concentrate and work away from the surrounding tumult of the executive offices. Grover Cleveland, Benjamin Harrison, FDR, and Harry Truman used it for this purpose. Franklin Roosevelt used it the most, often inviting advisers to stay for cocktails that he would mix himself, followed by dinner served on trays.

Here, the day after FDR's first inauguration, the president met with his cabinet to discuss the financial crisis and later signed the Emergency Banking Act of 1933. On December 7, 1941, at about 1:40 P.M., Roosevelt and Harry Hopkins were having lunch when a telephone call brought the news of the bombing of Pearl Harbor. On New Year's Day 1942, Roosevelt was joined in this room by Winston Churchill, Maxim Litvinof of the Soviet Union, and T.V. Soong representing China for the signing of an agreement to join with twenty-six countries in a "united nations" against Axis aggression. And the list goes on and on.

The room has also been, during John Adams' administration and then every one since Kennedy's, the parlor where the president and first lady entertain their guests of honor before official state functions. This invitation to "come upstairs" at the White House is one of the rarest and also most cherished. It is the presidential equivalent of inviting someone to your home, because the first floor of the White House is truly a public arena, and it is only upstairs that privacy prevails. The photographs of the Reagans and Gorbachevs drinking cocktails in the Yellow Oval Room are one more reflection of the end of the Cold War. President and Mrs. Clinton will welcome many more heads of former communist bloc countries and, standing by the tall windows, point out the memorial to the author of the Declaration of Independence and the monument to the father of the oldest continuous democracy in the world.

Woodrow Wilson, while working alone in this room during the dark days of World War I, would contemplate the painting on the far wall, "Signing of the Peace Protocol Between Spain and the United States, August 12, 1998" by Théobald Chartran. In it President McKinley stands at the end of the cabinet table that had served as his desk (and now serves as President Clinton's desk in this room). Just a few months earlier, on April 20, 1898, McKinley had regretfully signed the document authorizing military action in what John Hay called the "splendid little war" and which was the United States's first foray into imperialism beyond its shores.

Spectacular in both the full-size and miniature Treaty Rooms

is the chandelier. Approximately 250 hours of handwork went into making this chandelier for the White House replica. John Zweifel had to work with tiny tubing, brass rings, glass beading, and hair-thin copper wires for electrifying the lilliputian chandelier. Every glass shade had to be hand-blown by an expert who could measure his or her breath so that each one was exactly the same petite size as the preceding one.

The pewter inkwell stands just two inches high yet looks colossal the replica of the historic Treaty Room The full-size quill is eight inches long; the baby quill is $2/3$ inch.

Treaty Room

- *In 1809, it was a large bedroom.*
- *In 1823, James Monroe sat at a desk in this room and wrote his doctrine warning Europe to stay out of the Western Hemisphere.*
- *In 1825, John Quincy Adams made it a sitting room.*
- *From 1849 until the time of Lincoln's assassination it was a reception room for visitors wanting to see the president.*
- *In 1866, Andrew Johnson made it his cabinet room, and it functioned as such until the West Wing was built.*
- *In 1902, Theodore Roosevelt made it into a study. Woodrow Wilson spent most of his time in this room, where he wrote the Fourteen Points, his personal requirements for peace after World War I.*
- *In 1930, it became the "Monroe Drawing Room" after Mrs. Hoover placed reproduction Monroe furniture in it.*
- *In 1936, it was one of the rooms Eleanor Roosevelt used for press conferences.*
- *In 1945, Winston Churchill used it as his personal map room.*
- *In 1952, it was a sitting room.*
- *In 1962, Jacqueline Kennedy made it the Treaty Room (as seen in the photograph).*
- *In 1990, it became the president's office in the residence.*

In 1962, 80 million Americans watched the television tour of the White House and saw President and Mrs. Kennedy sitting in the Treaty Room answering Charles Collingwood's questions. Many of the questions referred to the changes Mrs. Kennedy was making to the White House. John Kennedy observed that every president who comes to live in the White House receives stimulus from the legendary figures who served in the same capacity. He explained: "Anything which dramatizes the great story of the United States—as I think the White House does—is worthy of the closest attention and respect by Americans who live here and who visit here and who are part of our citizenry. That's why I am glad that Jackie is making the effort she's making."[14]

The Treaty Room, recreated to resemble the Cabinet Room during Ulysses S. Grant's term of office and to commemorate peace treaties signed to end or prevent wars, was a Jacqueline Kennedy inspiration and realization. She was particularly proud of her research in tracking down the treaties signed in this room, and procuring facsimiles from the National Archives to hang on the walls.

Interior decorators could hardly believe Mrs. Kennedy was resurrecting Victorian furniture considered terribly unfashionable in 1962, but the first lady was far more interested in historical precedents than design magazine approval. Her passion during the three short years she lived in the White House was to imbue the house with the spirit of past presidents, and the Treaty Room was a fine example of her aspirations. The room is strikingly unified in design, and most of the furnishings originated with past presidents.

The White House television tour was a Jacqueline Kennedy tour de force with more than a little help from CBS, and she possessed star quality equal to her subject. She knew what to say on camera and how to

Almost all the furniture and wall treatments, except for the chandelier, were selected by Mrs. Kennedy in 1961 and 1962. The table, the sofa, the bentwood swivel armchair, and several upholstered chairs were purchased by President Grant in the 1870s. The table was used for cabinet meetings, and each secretary had his own drawer, which he could lock. The red rococo-revival armchair, seen reflected in the mirror purchased by Franklin Pierce, is similar to the chair Lincoln sat in for his famous portrait by George Healy, now in the State Dining Room. The torchères on either side of the mantel were a gift to President Jackson at the time of his inauguration in 1829. The heart-back chairs have been in the White House since the time of James Polk and have been used periodically in the dining rooms. The pattern of the geometric border is identical to the wallpaper in the room in the Peterson home across from Ford's Theatre, where Lincoln died.

President Grant looks down upon his furniture from a Henry Ulke portrait hung to the left of the mantel. Another great soldier, Zachary Taylor, in uniform, is on the right. One of the most moving paintings in the White House, titled *The Peacemakers,* by George Healy (not visible in the photograph), hangs on the wall opposite the fireplace. The painting shows Generals Sherman and Grant, President Lincoln, and Admiral Porter aboard the Union steamer *River Queen.* The wretched Civil War is coming to a close and they are discussing peace terms.

say it. A classic example of her tact and ability to find common ground with her audience was recorded in the published transcript of the program. Charles Collingwood asked Mrs. Kennedy what purpose the Treaty Room would serve, and the television audience heard her reply:

Well I do think every room should have a purpose. It can still be a sitting room because that sofa, though you may not believe it, will look nice. But it will serve a definite purpose. My husband has so many meetings up here in this part of the house. All the men who wait to see him now sit in the hall with the baby carriages going by them. They can sit in here and talk while waiting for him.

During the rehearsal period, however, when Mrs. Kennedy was asked why she was refurnishing the room, she replied, "It's really to get the Cabinet out of the living room."

Many presidents have used the old cabinet table that was the focal point of Mrs. Kennedy's restoration for the signing of peace treaties. William McKinley watched as the peace treaty ending the Spanish-American War was signed in August 1898; Calvin Coolidge in 1929 put his signature on the ratification of the Kellogg-Briand Peace Pact; John Kennedy, in 1963, signed the "Treaty for a Partial Nuclear Test Ban"; Richard Nixon, in 1972, signed the "Treaty of the Limitation of Anti-Ballistic Missile Systems"; in 1979 the table was taken outdoors for the momentous signing of the Egyptian-Israeli Peace Treaty by Menachem Begin, Anwar el-Sadat, and Jimmy Carter (see document page 193); and on a brilliant, sunny day in September 1993, the world witnessed not only the signing of the Israeli-Palestinian peace treaty on the cherished cabinet table, but also the handshake between Yitzak Rabin and Yasir Arafat that took place alongside that American heirloom.

The photograph above shows part of the former Treaty Room as it appears in the Clinton White House (except for the rug, which is not correct). The president uses the room as an office and the historic cabinet table (opposite page) as his desk. A child of the sixties, the president favors strong colors, but no one quite understands why the Clintons, whose love of American history spans the entire 200-year history of the house, have allowed a prevalence of Victoriana to dominate newly refurnished White House rooms. Clinton has kept the Chartran treaty painting (see page 72) and added ones of Benjamin Franklin and George Washington. Scattered throughout the room are the president's favorite photographs and mementos. The president's books flank the fireplace in bookcases built in situ by White House carpenters (see Carpenters' Shop, p.190) because they were too large to fit through the doorways. The overall effect resulting from the choice of fabrics, colors, lamps, and upholstered furniture is a reflection of the judgment of Little Rock interior decorator Kaki Hockersmith.

Mrs. Clinton, discussing the changes she is making to the White House, stated in an interview published in *Historic Preservation* (November–December 1993) that "preservation and restoration—not redecoration" is what she and her husband hope to achieve. "We're interested in enhancing the house and the furnishings within it . . . as a means of furthering the historical mission of the house." As President Clinton enjoys inviting certain guests and foreign dignitaries to his office in the residence, it, like other rooms, "should depict the quality and the importance of the White House as a living museum," asserts the first lady.

On the mantel, which has seen many decorators come and go, is carved the following: "This room was first used for meetings of the cabinet during the administration of President Johnson. It continued to be so used until the year MCMII. Here the Treaty of Peace with Spain was signed."

Charles McKim, President and Mrs. Theodore Roosevelt's architect and interior designer, wanted in 1902 to rid the White House of all the Victorian furniture. Edith Roosevelt insisted that certain pieces be kept, including the majestic carved rosewood bed now in the Lincoln Bedroom. Teddy Roosevelt subsequently enjoyed many restful nights in it; Woodrow Wilson, we assume, spent many restless nights worrying about World War I; and Calvin Coolidge remained silent on the subject of how he slept in the imposing Lincoln Bed. Had the architect instead of the first lady had his way, one of the most famous pieces of furniture in the White House might have been lost forever.

The elaborately carved Victorian table was also part of the furniture purchased by Mary Todd Lincoln from William and George Carryl of Philadelphia in 1861. In 1860, the prince of Wales stayed overnight in the "best guest room" in the James Buchanan White House, a room described by Mrs. Lincoln's cousin as "most shabby." The bed and the table reflect Mary Todd Lincoln's idea of appropriate furniture for a guest bedroom. In 1970, another prince of Wales, Prince Charles, slept in the bed that came to the White House as a result of his ancestor's brief visit.

The cream-colored silk sofa and matching chairs, believed to have been used in the White House during Lincoln's administration, were discovered in England and given to the White House in 1954. The "slipper" chair is upholstered in yellow and green William Morris fabric provided by a citizen who wanted to help Mrs. Kennedy with the restoration of the Lincoln Room.

The rocking chair (right foreground) is similar to the chair Lincoln used in the box at Ford's Theatre the night of his assassination. In front of the walnut bureau with full-length mirror, bought by Mary Lincoln, one nineteenth-century White House guest did her "pompadour every morning."

Visitors staying the night make certain to sit at the desk on the left. This has been authenticated as the desk Lincoln used at the "summer White House," a few miles northeast of 1600 Pennsylvania Avenue. The chairs at the desk and along the north wall were in Lincoln's cabinet room. The tables flanking the bed were purchased by President Jackson, whose portrait, seen to the left of the bed, hung in the exact spot when this room was Lincoln's office (see pages 108–11).

Lincoln Bedroom

The towering figure in the history of the White House was Abraham Lincoln. Theodore Roosevelt spoke for every chief executive when he said: "I think of Lincoln, shambling, homely, with his strong, sad, deeply-furrowed face, all the time. I see him in the different rooms and in the halls." The Lincoln Bedroom, which was the sixteenth president's office and cabinet room (see pages 108–11), is the only room in the White House named after and honoring a past president. Jacqueline Kennedy commented:

Sometimes I used to stop and think about it all. I wondered, "How are we going to live as a family in this enormous place?" I would go and sit in the Lincoln Room. It was the one room in the White House with a link to the past. It gave me great comfort. I love the Lincoln Room. Even though it isn't really Lincoln's bedroom, it has his things in it. When you see that great bed, it looks like a cathedral. To touch something I knew he had touched was a real link with him. The kind of peace I felt in that room was what you feel when going to church. I used to sit in the Lincoln Room and I could really feel its strength. I'd sort of be talking with him. Jefferson is the President with whom I have the most affinity. But Lincoln is the one I love.[15]

A plaque on the mantelpiece reads: "In this room Abraham Lincoln signed the Emancipation Proclamation of January 1, 1863 whereby four million slaves were given their freedom and slavery forever prohibited in these United States." This was an act of great personal courage and historic consequence. Even without the furniture, presidents entering the room feel the power of the past and the necessity of just leadership in the future.

The table stands less than 2 ½ inches high, but Jack Zweifel, John and Jan's eldest son, carved all the fine details found in the original piece. Storks support the marble surface, grapes hang down from the circular top, and the legs brace a bird's nest underneath. The rosewood table is the finest example of woodcarving in the White House replica. It took approximately 160 hours to carve and many hours to sand and stain. The Gettysburg Address, seen in facsimile in the background, is traditionally displayed in the Lincoln Bedroom in the form of a holographic copy.

Lincoln never slept in the 9-feet-long, 6-feet-wide bed that carries his name, but by its side he wept uncontrollably at the sight of his small son Willie, lost forever in its folds, dead at the age of eleven. Three years later, in 1865, the man who pleaded for "malice toward none; with charity for all" was embalmed at the foot of the big bed, shot by an assassin's bullet.

For many years, this room has been reserved for guests. FDR insisted that his close adviser Harry Hopkins and his new bride even live in the Lincoln suite (bedroom and sitting room), and had it repainted for them. Harry Truman, a passionate devotee of American history, decided to pull together furniture from Lincoln's time and place it here.

Lincoln Sitting Room

Located in the southeast corner of the mansion, this small room's moment of glory came during the McKinley administration and the Spanish-American War. The site of the president's "War Room," frequently referred to in histories of the war, is rarely specifically situated. But it was this small space that became, as William Seale says, "the lifeline of war communications . . . removing it from its traditional place in the War Department." In 1901, over the same telegraph lines, came the news that McKinley had been shot by an assassin while visiting the Pan-American Exposition in Buffalo. Colonel Crook, who had served as executive clerk at the White House since the early 1860s, remembered thinking as he read the telegram, "Good God! First Lincoln—then Garfield—and now McKinley!"

For the first quarter of the nineteenth century, the Lincoln Sitting Room was simply empty. When Charles Dickens visited the White House in the 1840s, it was Tyler's "unimpressive" office. Later, it was generally occupied by the president's private secretary and had the luxury of a water closet at the north end, contributing to its irregular shape. The room became the telegraph office during the administration of Rutherford B. Hayes. After the executive offices were moved out of the mansion in 1902, it was used by the first family themselves or as part of one of the principal guest suites in the house.

Richard Nixon read and listened to music here. He always liked a fire in the fireplace, even in summer, and, according to his daughter Tricia, had the air conditioning turned up to compensate for his idiosyncratic habit. John Zweifel included in his rendering of this room the cigar burns in the carpet that Nixon inadvertently caused.

Visitors to the White House replica often ask themselves, "What makes it look so real?" The answer lies in the thousands of little details. In this small room of the replica, there is a "fire" in the fireplace, and it flickers. The logs are perfectly scaled; even the knots are in proportion. All the necessary tools are there to maintain the fire, and the andirons have been perfectly shaped to fit the space. The mantel is a carved copy of the original. The picture frame and the wainscoting are built up from thin pieces of wood to look like the real thing. There is a copy of the painting *Pavilion at Gloucester* by William Glackens. The electrified candles burn, and although the copy of the French Empire clock on the mantel does not tick, other clocks in the White House replica do.

The decor dates from the Reagan administration. The desk on the right was made by James Hoban, the original architect of the White House. The four rosewood chairs were purchased by Mary Todd Lincoln. The plaster cast sculpture titled *Neighboring Pews* was created by John Rogers, the most popular sculptor in America between 1860 and 1895.

Queen's Bedroom and Sitting Room

Ike Hoover, who worked for ten presidents, described Will Rogers' visit to the Coolidge White House:

Mr. Rogers had been assigned to what is known as the pink [Queen's] guest suite, in the extreme north- east corner of the bedroom floor. It consists of a large room with a four-poster bed, a small dressing-room, which also has a single brass bed in it, and a private bath. He was escorted halfway down the hall by the President and his room pointed out to him. A door- man was summoned to have one last word with Mr. Rogers and learn if there was anything that could be done for him before he retired.

Upon entering the room, Mr. Rogers seemed rather hesitant about occupying the large four-poster bed that had been prepared for him. Turning to the doorman, he inquired if he had to sleep there. He was told of the small bed in the dressing-room and chose that in preference to the large one. The man turned down these covers and left Mr. Rogers with his own thoughts, to spend the night in the White House with all the thrills he afterwards described.[16]

Truman's mother couldn't see herself in this big, beautiful guest room (originally called the Rose Bed- room) either, declaring she would rather sleep on the floor. The bed was too high, the decor too fussy, she declared, and like the earthy humorist, she slept in the small sitting room. The entertainer Sammy Davis Jr., however, when he spent the night at the White House, turned down the chance to sleep in the famed Lincoln Bedroom in favor of the Queen's Bedroom. He later joked, "I thought to myself, now I don't want [Lin- coln] coming in here talking about 'I freed them, but I sure didn't mean for them to sleep in my bed.'"

The White House needed a sumptuous bedroom. Before Blair House, located across the street, became the official presidential guest house, the White House did have many overnight visitors with singularly imperious or peculiar ways. Winston Churchill and Madame Chiang Kai-shek during the war years were two of the most demanding. And royalty never fits smoothly into a household labeled the "first house of democracy." It is known that the White House staff were often disconcerted by the manner in which cer- tain supercilious guests ordered them about. Whether "Mr. Brown" (alias for V. M. Molotov, Soviet minis- ter for foreign affairs, who slept in the Rose Bedroom in 1942) addressed them as "comrade" has gone un- recorded. What *has* been recorded are the findings of the valet who unpacked Molotov's suitcase: black bread, sausages, and a revolver.

The Rose Bedroom was renamed the Queen's Bedroom by Jacqueline Kennedy in honor of the royal guests who had occupied it. Among these were Queen Elizabeth of Great Britain in 1942, Queen Wilhelmina of the Netherlands in 1942, Queen Julianna of the Netherlands in 1952, Queen Freder- ika of Greece in 1953, and Queen Elizabeth II of Great Britain in 1957.

In the days of Buchanan and Lincoln, the president's private secretaries lived in this bedroom, with twenty-four-hour dedication to the job expected. John Hay and John G. Nicolay shared the room in the 1860s. By the time of Andrew Johnson's presi- dency, his private secretary was moved to the corner room (today's Queen's Sitting Room), and the larger space became an office occupied by six clerks. When executive offices were finally built adjoining the man-

The Queen's Bedroom overlooks Lafayette Park to the north of the White House. The four-poster bed is thought to have belonged to Andrew Jackson; it came from the Hermitage, his home in Tennessee. The Federal sofa has scrolled arms and floral decorations on the top rail. The carved wood mantel on the west wall dates from the years 1820–30 and was removed from a Philadelphia house built in 1792. The English looking glass over the mantel with an eighteenth-century floral painting framed with it was presented to the White House by Princess (now Queen) Elizabeth on behalf of her father, King George, when she and Prince Philip visited Washington in 1951. The princess remarked that it was the king's "hope, and mine, that [the mirror] will remain here, as a mark of our friendship, so long as the White House shall stand."

The Queen's Bedroom has traditionally been given to female guests, as the Lincoln Bedroom was considered the more masculine. Female portraits, too, dominate the paintings in the room.

One of the most beautiful is of the actress Fanny Kemble (seen above the sofa). The artist, Thomas Sully, was the son of English actors who emigrated to America in 1792. Fanny Kemble also arrived in America from England with her actor father in 1832 and soon won the hearts of American audiences.

The actress was presented to Andrew Jackson at the White House in 1833, the year she married and gave up the stage. Vehemently opposed to the slavery she witnessed on her husband's Georgia plantation, she divorced him in 1849. She began to give public readings that became legendary. Longfellow was enraptured: "How our hearts glowed and trembled / as she read . . . " She also wrote *Journal of a Residence on a Georgian Plantation*, published in England in 1863, hoping to encourage a public outcry against slavery. Her nephew later married President Ulysses Grant's daughter Nellie in the Blue Room. Fanny is a favorite of first families and an inspiring companion while staying overnight at the White House.

Sir Winston Churchill spent a total of forty-two frenetic days at the White House, including nearly a month's stay shortly after Pearl Harbor. When he arrived, with an aide, secretary, two Scotland Yard men, and a valet, he virtually took over. Everyone in his entourage needed to sleep in close proximity to Churchill and consequently, because the house is not as large as many an English manor, near Roosevelt. Churchill occupied the Queen's Suite, opposite Harry Hopkins' room and down the corridor from the Roosevelts.

Stories of Churchill at the White House abound. Although there is no evidence that Eleanor bumped into him stark naked one night, David Eisenhower thought the story was worth investigating; he concluded, after conducting various interviews, that it would have been impossible. Winston Churchill II reported that his grandfather always slept in a vest (undershirt), nothing more, nothing less.

Legend has it that Franklin did get to see all of the prime minister. As the story goes, Churchill was dictating in his bath, and continued to dictate while walking around his room in a towel and even after the towel fell to the floor. It was then that Roosevelt entered the room and was greeted with the famous declaration: "The prime minister of Great Britain has nothing to hide from the president of the United States." But when Robert Sherwood, the playwright, author, and onetime speechwriter for FDR, asked Churchill if the story was true, the great statesman replied that it was not. He maintained that he always had his towel around his imposing belly.

Churchill stayed up nightly talking to the president until about 2:00 A.M. Roosevelt would attempt to put in normal working days, but Churchill, according to contemporary reports, spent a large part of the day "hurling himself violently in and out of bed, bathing at unsuitable moments and rushing up and down corridors in his dressing gown." If there hadn't been a war to win, Eleanor would have kicked him out. The cigar on the bed is a "Super Churchill," placed here for scale and not to suggest that the prime minister was careless about where he left his smoldering cigars.

sion during Teddy Roosevelt's tenure, the rows of desks that had filled this room for so many years were placed in a large room at the west end of the West Wing. This room then became the Rose Bedroom and the site of Alice Roosevelt Longworth's childhood appendectomy.

Today, the Queen's Bedroom and Lincoln Bedroom accommodate personal friends and family of the president and first lady who are invited to spend the night at the best address in the country.

The *Architectural Digest* (December 1981) described the Queen's Sitting Room as "evoking a stately yet festive tone." French fabric with a neoclassical medallion design was installed during the Kennedy administration. A draped dressing table is festooned with tasseled cord. The crown and scepter are just for fun, reminding the viewer that the White House replica descends from a long line of magnificent miniatures, including Queen Mary's Dolls' House at Windsor Castle.

Movie Theater in East Colonnade

In July 1942, President Franklin Roosevelt ordered the White House cloakroom, located in the east colonnade, converted into a movie theater. From that time on, the White House has had no permanent coatroom, but every first family would probably agree that having a personal movie theater is better. In any case, the space still serves as the temporary coatroom.

As early as 1933, Roosevelt was receiving newsreel footage of important presidential activities. The president also was sent copies of films made by government agencies and, once the war began, many of the propaganda films. Family and friends have probably used the theater far more than the president, especially since the White House also has always had access to feature films.

Margaret Truman was delighted to learn that she could ask for a viewing of any Hollywood movie, new or old, at any time she desired. It is reported that she saw her favorite, *The Scarlet Pimpernel*, sixteen times. Mamie Eisenhower, like many American women in the 1950s, enjoyed watching a movie on a Saturday afternoon. She was particularly fond of sharing the sixty-five-seat theater with her young grandchildren. Her husband, too, watched many movies there. Presidents Carter and Reagan normally waited until they were resting at Camp David to savor Hollywood's latest offerings. President Clinton's "favorite cultural activity," noted the *New York Times* on March 23, 1994, "seems to be showing movies at the White House."

The East Garden, better known as the Jacqueline Kennedy Garden, is both more public and more private than its companion, the Rose Garden, to the west. The million and a half visitors who come each year to the White House have the opportunity of viewing it on the public tour. After passing the security check in the East Wing lobby, visitors proceed to the Garden Room and then through the glass-enclosed colonnade that runs along the north side of the garden.

But come the afternoon, after the last public visitor has been politely ushered out of the White House by the Secret Service and the German shepherd that always brings up the rear, the first lady, her family, and guests have this congenial garden as their outdoor retreat. One hundred people may be greeting the president in the Rose Garden, but the Jacqueline Kennedy Garden is off-limits and tranquil.

The massive renovation of the White House that took place during the Truman administration left the gardens in shambles, as anyone who has had concrete mixers and bulldozers drive through their backyard could predict. Shrubbery was planted during the Eisenhower administration, but the Kennedys wanted attractive, colorful gardens to look out onto. They asked Rachel Lambert Mellon, a personal friend but not a professional landscape architect, to design the gardens to the southwest and southeast of the mansion.

Jacqueline Kennedy Garden

The East Garden was named the Jacqueline Kennedy Garden in 1963 by Lady Bird Johnson in tribute to her predecessor's contribution in promoting gardening at the White House. It features a pergola at one end (photograph at left) and a fountain (photograph at right) at the other. In the White House replica, a pump sends water up through the miniature fountain all day long. In the photograph a true-size golf ball stamped "General Ike" supports a miniaturized set of golf clubs that are personalized "Ford."

The Rose Garden and the Jacqueline Kennedy Garden are both approximately 100 feet long and 50 feet wide. Mrs. Mellon designed them so that a central quadrangle of grass is surrounded by hedge, flowers, and trees. The magnolias and flowering crab apples in the Rose Garden and the topiary in the Jacqueline Kennedy Garden are only two of the many variations on Mrs. Mellon's basic geometric design that give the two gardens their distinct qualities.

Calligraphers' Office

This large office on the second floor of the East Wing is known both as the Calligraphers' Office and by its official title, the Social Entertainments Office. The responsibilities of the men and women who work here extend beyond expert lettering. They design the White House invitations, programs, Christmas and other cards, special awards, certificates, and menus, and do other projects on behalf of the president and first lady. They work to maintain the highest standards in design and in protocol. A mistake arising in this office could mean an affront to a monarch, head of state, Hollywood star, sports hero, political bigwig, or excited John Doe.

When the approved guest list for a White House function is sent here, the staff must make absolutely certain that the guest listed is the guest invited. This office is given only the guests' names, and it is then the responsibility of the staff to find the correct addresses. They also confirm spelling, full titles, and abbreviations. Everything must be exact; mistakes reflect on the presidency.

Russell Armentrout, a graphic designer and former head of this department, worked here from the Eisenhower into the Carter administrations. He remembers when guest lists for state functions were sent to newspapers in order of protocol. He and his staff had to get the order correct. Now the names are listed alphabetically, a job any computer is perfectly capable of doing, and a modification of which Thomas Jefferson, if not the diplomatic corps, would approve.

A White House invitation reads, "The President and Mrs. Clinton Request the Pleasure of the Company of ————." A calligrapher writes the name of the guest and sometimes the date, matching the lettering, which has been engraved at the Bureau of Engraving and Printing. Of course, for a reception where the numbers would prohibit this personal touch, the invitation would say, "President and Mrs. Clinton request the pleasure of your company." Each envelope, addressed by hand in "social handwriting," takes about two minutes to do. For a state dinner, 140 may be invited to dine, but twice that many may receive invitations for "music" in the East Room after dinner.

Most people respond in the affirmative to an invitation to dine at the White House. It is generally considered the hottest ticket not just in town, but in the nation. Once the responses have been received, the Social Office proceeds to make up the "escort" envelopes that will be handed to the guests after they have checked their coats and ascended the stairs to the state floor. The envelope contains a card giving the guest his or her table number. On the tables are the hand-lettered place cards and menus. The programs for the evening's entertainment are passed out as guests enter the East Room from the State Dining Room.

Rose Garden and West Colonnade

A perk of the presidency is being able to walk to work. Generally the president comes down from the second floor in the elevator, passes along the ground-floor (the original basement) corridor and garden room, and then walks along the west colonnade or through the Rose Garden to the Oval Office. White House chief usher Ike Hoover described another route that presidents sometimes took. This he characterized as the "overland route" because the chief executive left the mansion through the French doors of the State Dining Room (center of photograph), and walked via the west terrace (over colonnade) and down a flight of winding steps directly into the executive offices. The "subway route," as Ike Hoover called the first one, originally passed through some quite shabby areas of the mansion, and many first ladies thought it was undignified for their husbands to be walking past the laundry and servant quarters on their way to the office.

The oval painting, seen through the double doors leading to the Rose Garden, is a powerfully uplifting canvas viewed regularly by the president on the subway route. Titled *Union*, it was painted by Constantino Brumidi in 1869. Art historian William Kloss describes the female subject as "the flag personified" in her flowing red, white, and blue garments. Floating upward, she looks to the heavens and thirteen stars. She raises above her a shield with red and white stripes and is supported by an American bald eagle (the symbol of authority) holding arrows (signifying preparedness) and an olive branch (symbolizing peace). She wears a Phrygian, or liberty, cap—a symbol of freedom through revolution.

The president often passes the spot where in the photograph sits a potted plant under a large tree. On October 13, 1992, the two-hundredth anniversary of the laying of the cornerstone of the White House, a time capsule was sealed and buried at this site.

The contents of the time capsule include the following:

- *President and Mrs. Bush's schedules for October 13, 1992*
- *A presidential proclamation in celebration of the two-hundredth anniversary of the White House*
- *The flag flown over the White House July 17–October 13, 1992*
- *Paint chips from the exterior restoration of 1980–1992*
- USA Today *and* The Washington Post, *for October 13, 1992*
- *The commemorative White House issue of* Life *magazine, November 1992 (which includes a double-page picture of the White House replica)*
- *A videotape giving the history of the White House*
- *Computer disks containing the 1991 White House inventory*
- *The current executive residence staff roster*
- *A White House grounds brochure*
- The White House: An Historic Guide
- *A U.S. Treasury Department engraving and die of the White House*
- *A copy of* Millie's Book, *signed by Barbara Bush*
- *A White House commemorative stamp, coin, and Christmas ornament*
- *A Bush family photo, Bush/Gorbachev watch, Bush pen*
- *Seeds from the magnolia tree planted during Andrew Jackson's administration*

It has not been announced when the capsule will be opened. But whether it is October 13, 2092, or October 13, 2192, and whether or not our descendants will be able to use the videotape or computer disk, each president of the United States is responsible for keeping the world safe until then.

a.

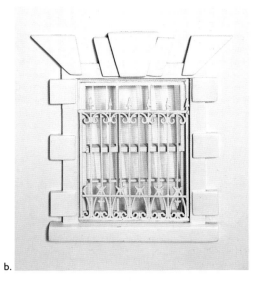

b.

c.

d.

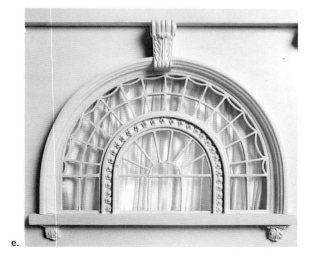

e.

Architectural Details

a. The entablature of the White House consists of its architrave, dentils, modillions, and overhanging cornice. Above this is the stone balustrade composed of piers, round balusters, and top rail.

b. A copy of a typical basement window on the north wall. Carving the projecting voussoir stones was a complex task for even the skilled stonemasons building the president's house in the late 1700s. Bars have been attached to the windows since the 1820s to protect the house and the stores of silver, liquor, and food.

c. The White House is considered the finest eighteenth-century stone house in the United States. The stone carving surrounding the north doorway is the most intricate and complex expression of the craft as executed in the 1790s in America. Above the entrance are high-relief carvings of ribbons, bows, and swags of oaks leaves and acorns accented with the glorious stone roses that are a recurring motif on the exterior White House walls.

d. James Hoban, the White House architect, designed both the north and south porticos at the time the house was rebuilt in 1817–18 after the British had burned it. It was not, however, until 1824 that the south portico was completed and 1829 that the north portico, with its porte-cochère, was erected.

e. One of two large lunette windows that provide the second-floor transverse corridor in the family quarters with exquisite light. The west window is the centerpiece of the family living room. The east window lights the hallway between the Queen's and Lincoln Bedroom suites.

A quiet doorway below some high-powered offices in the West Wing. The Yale key with the words "White House" is a reproduction of the key presented to Harry Truman on April 23, 1952, upon the completion of the renovation of the White House. Along with the key, the following inscription was presented to the president, "In a free society, the key to a man's house symbolizes his and his family's rights to those privacies and freedoms which are at the heart and sinews of the American way of life." Harry Truman used to say that the "American way of life" could be summed up in the Bill of Rights and the idea that there should be equal opportunity for everybody to make a "living." After that, Truman said, "Most Americans want to own their own house and lot, or a small farm, and then raise a family."

f.

f. The Palladian entry, centered on the west wall, provides access from the State Dining Room to the top of the west colonnade where, in the nineteenth century, there had been greenhouses and a conservatory. On fine summer evenings, tables are sometimes set up on the terrace, and the president and his guests dine in the open air.

West Wing

A view of the White House from the west wall of the West Wing looking east. One of the pleasures of studying the White House replica is seeing angles and aspects of White House architecture you can never observe on a visit to Washington.

Each administration designates which official will occupy a particular office in the West Wing. The lit windows in the photograph are often the offices of, from left to right, the national security adviser (once Henry Kissinger's office), the vice-president, a secretary, and the chief of staff. The guard box on the left is a holdover from World War II, when security was tightened and never subsequently relaxed.

Teddy Roosevelt's large and rambunctious young brood provided the impetus to finally move the executive offices out of the first family's living quarters. The Roosevelts simply did not have enough bedrooms when half the second floor was official office space. In June 1902, the Sundry Civil Act provided money "for a building to accommodate the offices of the President, to be located in the grounds of the Executive Mansion."

The West Wing was originally conceived as a temporary structure. The architects, McKim, Mead & White, however, fulfilled their objective, to "discover the design and intention of the original builders, and to adhere strictly thereto," in such an extraordinary way that their West Wing has remained. Intelligently and handsomely designed, the West Wing is hardly visible from the street. President Taft added the Oval Office (see pages 112–13), taking the elliptical shape of three favorite rooms in the mansion, and both Hoover and Franklin Delano Roosevelt, who moved the Oval Office to its present location near the Rose Garden, created more space for offices. But always, the two wings of the White House have blended architecturally with the main structure and shown a dignified subordination to the house that George Washington esteemed.

West Wing, Corner Office

The occupant of this corner office abutting the west colonnade takes a lot of the heat off the president. No wonder the space seems to glow with its own radiant energy. Even if it is cold outside, it can be very hot in here.

The office is normally occupied by the White House spokesperson or press secretary. He or she need only walk around the corner to the Press Briefing Room to report on the day's events and answer journalists' questions. The tiny televisions in the replica, each a mere 1 ½ inches high, really do work. When John Zweifel first built his model White House, he constructed an elaborate system of mirrors to reflect and reduce a large TV image to small scale. Television sets were strapped and squeezed into the underbelly of the replica. Today, he uses the portable televisions designed to be handheld, a technological breakthrough not available in the 1960s when he first thought to have working televisions as part of his White House miniature.

Press Briefing Room

The press corps did not always consider the White House a hot spot for news. Until 1896, reporters looked elsewhere in Washington for fast-breaking stories. During the Spanish-American War, there were finally enough journalists hanging around the White House to make it necessary for President McKinley to give daily briefings.

Teddy Roosevelt, McKinley's successor, had a good rapport with the press, and journalists were generally kind to him. Of course, he screened the newspapermen he allowed in for press conferences, and their admittance was based on whether or not he liked their stories. Teddy believed that journalists covering the White House fulfilled a "public service" and was the first president to set aside space specifically for them *inside* the White House.

Today, 1,700 people hold White House press credentials and the White House Briefing Room with its blue curtains is familiar to millions of Americans via television. The room seats sixty to seventy reporters, but when there is a big news story, dozens more squeeze in standing. Reagan, who wanted to make it easier for himself to remember journalists' names, assigned seats to certain members of the press.

According to legend, Richard Nixon strolled into the press's work space in the White House one Sunday morning in 1969 and could hardly believe how cramped and unattractive it was. If creating more congenial facilities could make the press friendlier, he was ready to find funds for this purpose.

The space Nixon allocated for the news media was in the west colonnade. Here Franklin Delano Roosevelt had built his indoor swimming pool, thanks in part to the contributions of nickels and

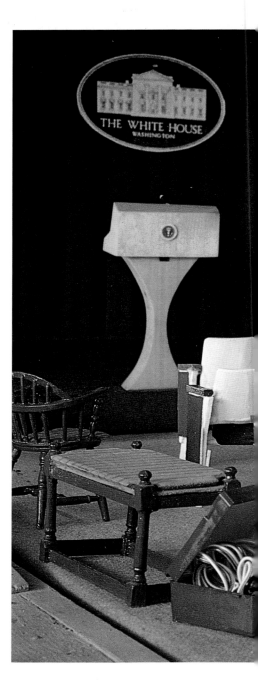

In 1969, under President Nixon, the press were given cubicles next to the Press Briefing Room equipped with telephones, radios, and work surfaces. Technology has outpaced even the fast-fixing Zweifel family. The White House miniature has yet to switch from manual typewriters to laptop computers.

dimes from America's schoolchildren and "the man on the street." New York newspapers led the campaign to build the pool to help ease the pain of the native son in the White House suffering from poliomyelitis.

Digging the White House pool revealed, according to William Seale, "the floor of the old stable from James Monroe's time about four feet down, its brick pavers and gutters intact." The present press corps should always remember this historic fact: they are *above* the gutter.

The television networks keep their cameras on a raised platform at the rear of the Press Briefing Room. The TV camera in the picture, not including the needle-thin tripod, is 1 1/2 inches long by 1/2 inch high.

Cabinet Room

The most celebrated conference room in the United States faces the most prestigious garden in the country. The Cabinet Room, nestled between the office of the president's personal secretary (which is adjacent to the Oval Office) and the Press Briefing Room, looks out over the Rose Garden. The room is simply furnished with an enormous mahogany pedestal table purchased by President Nixon in 1970 and large leather chairs, each having a brass plate designating the cabinet member who sits there during meetings. An ultimate White House "souvenir" is a Cabinet Room chair, normally purchased by the cabinet member's staff for their boss upon his or her leaving office.

Each president chooses the paintings to be hung here, and normally Washington or Lincoln can be found monitoring discussions. Woodrow Wilson held the place of honor over the mantel when Harry Truman took the presidential oath in this room at 7:08 P.M. on April 12, 1945. Members of the cabinet, Mrs. Truman, daughter Margaret, and many other officials were packed together to witness the one-minute swearing in.

Although the cabinet has met in the West Wing since 1902, this room began to be used as a cabinet meeting room only in 1934. A year later, as part of the New Deal, Roosevelt signed the Social Security Act in the new Cabinet Room. Like Social Security, the topics of the discussions that take place here affect the lives of every American. The weight on the shoulders of each cabinet member is immense, and the chairs appear to be designed to help take some of the strain. The chairs occupied by the president and vice-president are, symbolically, even larger. In the White House miniature, the chairs are cast iron. The table is 23 inches long.

Patio

On a fine day, the president may read documents, hold informal meetings, or have a meal on this patio just outside the Oval Office. Many historic photographs come to mind of presidents also relaxing in this area next to the Rose Garden. The most compelling image, though, is that of President Kennedy pacing behind the august columns, alone and with his advisers, during the Cuban missile crisis.

The tiny garden furniture is made of wire with dabs of fiberglass. Autumn leaves surround the 3-inch-high mock wrought-iron chairs.

Abraham Lincoln's Office and Oval Offices

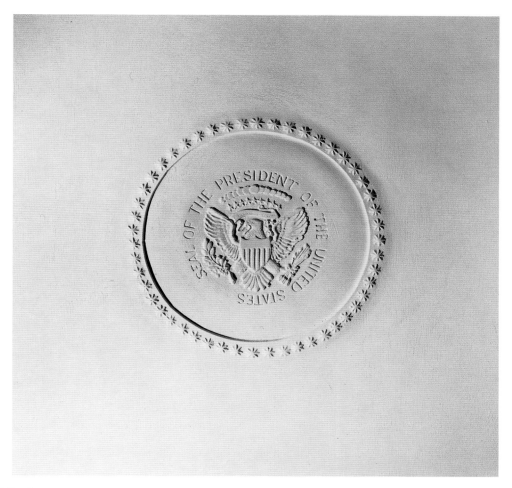

Presidential Seal

On the dome ceiling of the Oval Office, not visible in any of the photographs other than the above, is the presidential seal in plaster relief. Harry Truman established by executive order a legal definition of what the seal and the president's coat of arms should look like. Although both had been used since 1880, there was no known basis in law until 1945. The seal had originated during the administration of President Hayes, apparently as an erroneous rendering of the Great Seal of the United States.

The Great Seal of the United States was established in 1782, predating the Constitution, and is familiar to every American; it appears on the dollar bill. The American bald eagle, symbolizing authority, is prepared for both war and peace, holding in its talons the symbols for both. Truman wanted to ensure that the American eagle on the presidential seal would never again face the arrows of war, as sometimes it had, and that its head would always be turned toward the olive branch of peace.

Abraham Lincoln's Office
Sixteenth President
1809–1865

Even before John Zweifel began his thirty-year-plus marathon to build the White House replica, he was engaged in reproducing famous scenes and great moments in early American history. In the 1950s, one of his dreams (dreams *are* the impetus for all he does; practicality is hardly an ingredient of magic) was to recreate famous rooms from the Lincoln White House. The source material, however, did not exist; no one had bothered to document the house's furnishings at the time of Lincoln.

The result of Zweifel's research, after the frustration subsided, was a twofold commitment: to document (inch by inch) how the physical White House looked in his own time (see "A Gift to the People" for the complete story) and to make the one sketch that did exist of a room in the Lincoln White House into a diorama, with all the details and textures that would transport the viewer back in time.

The little-known sketch they discovered, by C. K. Stellwagen, showed Lincoln's office, which also served as the Cabinet Room. The sketch identified certain objects in the room and included a description of the color of the wallpaper. Lincoln signed the Emancipation Proclamation here. This room, therefore, would be worthy of the months and years of research and work ahead of John, now with the help of Jan. The Kunhardts, distinguished Lincoln historians, described Lincoln's office as follows:

Here, between these four walls, was the heart of the government of the United States. Here came the generals and admirals to report upon the progress of the war and give their recommendations; the senators and congressmen to make known their opinions, needs, desires; office seekers by the droves, waving their petitions, spouting credentials . . . Here came the inventors whose schemes and tinkerings, Lincoln was aware, could alter the future. Here came fiery people pleading causes, relatives of condemned men seeking pardons, widows searching for solace . . . Here came old friends and Indians, and the just plain curious. "They don't want much," said Lincoln. "They get but little, and I must see them."[17]

John Zweifel had the skill, honed since childhood, to recreate Lincoln's office and bring it to life.

Lincoln's office was the room now called the Lincoln Bedroom. In the time of the sixteenth president, the view to the south was of a partially completed Washington Monument, swamps, and open spaces. Inside the room, clutter prevailed, with only the high postmaster's desk with its alphabetized cubbyholes giving some semblance of order. Wall maps showed the location of the armies and battles of the Civil War. A rope pull (near the window on the right) summoned Lincoln's secretaries and servants.

Beside the large Victorian table, in July 1862, Lincoln formally proposed freeing all slaves. On January 1, 1863, the Emancipation Proclamation was laid on the table for his signature.

Every New Year's Day, the doors to the White House were opened for diplomats, military officers, and then the public to greet the president and shake his hand. On this New Year's Day in 1863, news of the imminent signing of the Emancipation Proclamation had spread, and people were already celebrating a moral victory at a time of dehumanizing bloody battles. The lines of people waiting to see the president were exceptionally long—and gay.

Lincoln returned to his office in the afternoon to await the delivery of the document. Secretary of State William Seward and his son collected the parchment from the calligrapher and brought it to the president. Lincoln raised his silvery steel pen, dipped it in the ink, and proclaimed: "I never in my life felt more certain that I was doing right, than I do in signing this paper. But I have been receiving calls and shaking hands since nine o'clock this morning, till my arm is stiff and numb.

"Now this signature is one that will be closely examined. If they find my hand trembled they will say, 'he had some complications.' But anyway, it is going to be done."[18]

Abraham Lincoln later declared that the Emancipation Proclamation was "the central act of my administration, and the great event of the nineteenth century."

William Howard Taft
Twenty-seventh President
1909–13

William Howard Taft was the only president to serve after his term of office as chief justice of the Supreme Court, a position he found preferable to the presidency.

Through much of the nineteenth century, presidents noted, some more vocally than others, that having the executive offices of government situated on the same floor as the first family's living quarters was not ideal. Theodore Roosevelt did more than grumble; he took action. In 1902, he got Congress to appropriate $65,195 for new offices on the west side of the mansion. When the New York architects McKim, Mead, and White and President Roosevelt could not agree on a design, they decided to construct a "temporary" building.

By 1909, still more office space for the president and his staff was needed. A competition was held to convert the "temporary" building into a permanent structure and to enlarge it. While President Taft took his summer vacation, the West Wing was nearly doubled in square footage, and an "Oval Office" for the president was added in the center. On September 5, a headline in the *New York Times* read: "WHITE HOUSE REFORMS: Where Once Was Tennis New Regime Brings in Reign of Typewriters." The tennis courts had been sacrificed in the name of more efficient government. Taft was the first president to go daily to the Oval Office, designed by the architect Nathan C. Wyeth to emulate the popular Blue Room.

Many changes were made to the West Wing over the years, but the president's office, except for being moved to its present position overlooking the Rose Garden, has remained the same. The architecture of the room is Colonial, or perhaps technically Federal Revival. The president's desk faces the marble mantel, three tall windows behind him bathing him in light.

The simple wood trim repeats itself over windows and doors, balanced by the modest, yet refined, wainscoting. In the Taft Oval Office, the walls were covered with green burlap, the woodwork painted white, and the furniture covered in caribou hide rubbed with red dye.

Today, the Oval Office is the most distinguished office in the world, and anyone would feel honored to be invited in. Taft, however, as the first president to work outside the traditional White House rooms, felt that his new office was not prestigious enough for certain ceremonial functions. He would not meet important dignitaries in the office, nor sign bills into law.

John Fitzgerald Kennedy
Thirty-fifth President
1961–63

President Kennedy cherished the old desk. Known as the *Resolute* desk, it had, in another life, sailed the seas. In 1852, the British barque-rigged ship *The Resolute* was sent to find missing Arctic explorers, but it was abandoned by its crew. American whalers later discovered the ship, and it was purchased, fitted, and restored by the American government and sent to Queen Victoria as a gift from the president and the American people. When the ship was finally broken up, her timbers were carved into this elaborate desk, which was presented to President Rutherford Hayes by Queen Victoria in 1879 as "a memorial of the courtesy and loving kindness which dictated the offer of the gift of the RESOLUTE."

On Kennedy's desk are the following items: the coconut shell with the call for rescue he inscribed after his PT boat was sunk by a Japanese destroyer in the Solomons during World War II; bookends that are replicas of *Old Ironsides'* cannons; books that variously included five of his own, Churchill's four-volume biography of Marlborough, Bemis' two-volume study of John Quincy Adams, Agar's *The Price of Union*, and Stendhal's *The Red and the Black*; items of nineteenth-century scrimshaw (carvings by sailors on ivory and whalebone); a desk set presented by Charles de Gaulle; and a plaque with the Breton fisherman's prayer "O, God, Thy sea is so great, and my boat is so small." The globe behind the desk was a gift from Admiral Arleigh Burke, and a daily source of reference for the president and a teaching tool for his children on their frequent visits to their father's office.

The needlepoint pillow with its native Greek design is a reproduction of the pillow that rested on President Kennedy's rocking chair in the Oval Office. Mrs. Kennedy purchased the original while on a trip to Greece in 1961. The middle ship in the group of three is a reduced copy of the model of the American steam and sail whaler given to President Kennedy by Nikita Khrushchev after the Vienna summit in 1961. The original was carved from whalebone and walrus tusk by a Chukchi craftsman. Although Kennedy and Khrushchev disagreed in Vienna on almost every important issue, the model ship was an inspired gift on the part of the Communist leader to his young adversary.

The famous porch rocker had been previously used by Kennedy in his Senate office. The cushions were a gift from the crew of the USS *Kitty Hawk* and the Commander Carrier Division One. Almost all the paintings in the room are associated with naval history, and the model ships around the room were prize possessions of the president.

Lyndon Baines Johnson

**Thirty-sixth President
1963–69**

Marble-top coffee table with telephone in drawer.

Lyndon Baines Johnson was a big man from a big state. He replaced Kennedy's *Resolute* desk with a larger, plainer one, removed the watercolors and naval paintings, and placed family photographs around the room. He even brought in a rocking chair of his own.

"High tech" defined the Johnson Oval Office. He liked buzzers, bells, and buttons. He liked telephones within reach. An aide once said, "If there was a phone call for him and there wasn't a phone beside wherever he was sitting, he'd say, 'Have one put in.'" Johnson would watch the news simultaneously on all three networks while working at his desk. And he wanted to receive the messages from the wire services pronto. He was the only president to have a teletype in the Oval Office (the teletype cabinet is next to the bank of television sets). After he made a major announcement, he would keep an eye on the teletype to learn the response from around the world.

Many times Johnson spoke to the nation from the Oval Office. The turmoil, tension, and disappointment of the "days of rage" could be measured on his face. On March 31, 1968, there came over television the indelible image of LBJ, forever fixed behind his big desk in the Oval Office, with a sadness even his diehard enemies could comprehend:

Tonight I want to speak to you of peace in Vietnam and Southeast Asia. No other question so preoccupies our people . . .

In the hope that this action will lead to early talks, I am taking the first step to de-escalate the conflict. We are reducing—substantially reducing—the present level of hostilities . . .

With America's sons in the fields far away, with America's future under challenge right here at home, with our hopes and the world's hopes for peace in the balance every day, I do not believe that I should devote an hour or a day of my time to any personal partisan causes or to any duties other than the awesome duties of this office—the Presidency of our country.

Accordingly, I shall not seek, and I will not accept, the nomination of my party for another term as your President.

Richard Milhous Nixon
Thirty-seventh President
1969–74

A "Memorandum for the President" dated Monday, 10:00 A.M., November 10, 1969, was sent from Dwight L. Chapin, Nixon's personal aide, to the president. Titled "Objects in Your Office," it read, in part, as follows:

You may be interested in the following information on objects which are now in your office:

18th century English cartel (wall) clock made by Job Tripp, circa 1775.

One pair of mahogany commode pedestals, circa 1805.

One pair of lamps, converted from Delft vases, made in Holland, circa 1760.

Collection of porcelain birds created by Edward Marshall Boehm.

Four silver sweetmeat dishes made by F. W. Cooper of New York, 1846.

Portrait of George Washington by Gilbert Stuart.

Marble top pier table of French origin, circa 1820.

Nixon was fastidious about what and where objects were placed in the Oval Office. Memoranda to and from H. R. Haldeman in 1969 show Nixon concerned about the placement of the coffee table so as not to block his view of the fireplace from his desk; the height for the portrait of George Washington in relationship to the clock; the position on the wall of the photograph of the moon given to the president by the lunar-landing astronauts.

Nixon's Oval Office was more ceremonial than utilitarian and thus the "look" was perhaps of more importance to him than to previous and later chief executives. The colors he chose, royal blue and gold, gave the office a regal appearance. With his "work-ing" office in the Executive Office Building to the west of the White House, the Oval Office was reserved for formal occasions.

William Safire in his book *Before the Fall: An Inside View of the Pre-Watergate White House* (1975) discusses the provenance of the desk Nixon used in the Oval Office and the problems that arose because of a misattribution. When Nixon was vice-president, he enjoyed using what was known as the "Wilson" desk in his office at the Capitol. When he became president, he requested the same massive desk and, according to Safire, "used it hundreds of times to get into points about idealism, about how Presidents can be misunderstood, how peaceful men find themselves with need to do battle, how the distinction between men of thought and men of action can no longer be drawn, etc."

The problem was, as an earnest researcher discovered, that the "Wilson" of the desk was not Woodrow but Henry, vice-president during the administration of Ulysses S. Grant. According to Safire, the lesser-known Wilson was distinguished in his own right—he was an early abolitionist, one of the founders of the Republican Party, etc.—but still, Nixon was disappointed, and not entirely convinced that the underling, who had done such a thorough job of interviewing knowledgeable individuals, comparing historical photographs, and tracking receipts, was correct. In any case, whatever the provenance of the desk, it was there that Nixon installed five hidden microphones (two more were hidden across the room in light sconces near the fireplace) that picked up everything he said about the desk—and a great deal more besides!

Gerald Rudolph Ford
Thirty-eighth President
1974–77

Gerald Ford became president under the most disturbing and difficult circumstances. Perhaps interior design does not often reflect political philosophy, but Gerald Ford knew he wanted the Oval Office redecorated, and he knew how. A press announcement in November 1974 stated that the Ford Oval Office would have a "warmer feeling" than Nixon's. The room was painted an off-white, and the upholstery was in shades of salmon, gold, and green. Mrs. Ford selected the design of the rug, deliberately avoiding presidential symbols and settling on a floral motif around the border. Gerald Ford continued to use the desk Richard Nixon had used, but removed the microphones.

Joining the perennial presidential favorites, the portrait of George Washington by Charles Wilson Peale over the mantel and "Bronco Buster" by Frederic Remington on a side table, were many fine paintings and sculptures chosen by President Ford for his office. Among these were "City of Washington, 1833 From Beyond the Navy Yard" by George Cooke which shows the sparse District of Columbia with the young White House and Capitol prominent; a nineteenth-century painting titled "Passing the Outpost" by A. Wordsworth Thompson which depicts American women delaying British soldiers so that their husbands, revolutionaries, may escape; and the 1929 bronze, "Abraham Lincoln: The Hoosier Youth" by Paul Manship.

The ship's wheel near Ford's desk is from the *Mayaguez*, the American merchant vessel seized by the Cambodians in 1975. The wheel was removed when the ship and its crew reached port safely after

The minuscule pipes rest in a miniature copy of the pipe rack handmade in Cantù, Italy, and presented to President Ford by President Giovanni Leone of Italy. Ford kept it in the Oval Office along with the pipe rack given to him by Leonid Brezhnev, general secretary of the USSR.

the rescue. The release of the crew after being taken hostage was one of the most joyous moments of Ford's presidency. The actual wheel is 44 inches wide and weighs 50 pounds.

At the Gerald Ford Presidential Library in Ann Arbor, Michigan, there is a lifesize replica of his Oval Office. An Oval Office exhibit is a popular feature at the Kennedy, Johnson, Carter, and Reagan presidential libraries in Boston, Austin, Atlanta, and Simi Valley, California, respectively.

James Earl Carter, Jr.
Thirty-ninth President
1977–81

In 1979, Jimmy Carter acquired for the White House collection the Charles Willson Peale portrait of George Washington that hangs over the mantel in the Oval Office. Washington was deeply engaged in planning the Revolutionary War and gave the artist only two sittings. But what a moment to catch the man who would become the father of the nation! The Declaration of Independence had only recently been written and signed. Washington stands contemplative and physically robust; he wears the light blue sash of commander in chief. Behind him lies Boston, with Beacon Hill prominent and Charlestown burning. Personal courage, moral intelligence, and a vision of a great, democratic nation define Washington in 1776. It is no wonder that the men who succeeded him as commander in chief wanted to have the portrait across from their desk. When they look up, Washington looks back.

When another type of inspiration was needed, Carter turned to his black Bible, which he kept in the Oval Office. His desk was relatively clear, although he liked the glass donkey kicking up its heels, presented to him by the Georgia Democratic Party. Margaret Truman Daniel gave him a replica of "The Buck Stops Here" sign that her father had kept on his desk.

A favorite object in the Carter Oval Office and in John Zweifel's replica is a glass-encased ship model (not visible in the photograph) behind Carter's desk. To make the miniature ship took one craftsman four eight-hour days. To work on such a small scale, surgical and dental tools, tweezers, an Exacto knife, and epoxy glue were used. Sutures, nylon thread pulled from curtains, and hairs extracted from paint brushes were turned into ropes and stays.

A miniature oil painting (3 7/8 by 3 1/8 inches) after the Charles Willson Peale portrait of George Washington. The painting was copied by Peale in November 1776 from the original he had done from life a few months earlier. The above is a brilliant example of a miniaturist's skill. Minuscule paintbrushes, wee dabs of paint, a steady hand, and paced breaths were required to execute the mini-masterpiece.

Ronald Wilson Reagan
Fortieth President
1981–89

Until Reagan became president, the Oval Office did not have a proper wood floor. In 1982, a walnut and white oak floor was laid, replacing a wood-grain vinyl installed in 1969 during the Nixon administration. That, in turn, replaced a cork flooring laid in Franklin Roosevelt's new office in 1934. Who would have thought, with America's vast timberland, that the presidents of the United States walked on cork and vinyl floors all those years?

The bronze miniature saddles and the jelly beans were items in the Reagan Oval Office that drew attention. The colorful ones, with the soft centers, need no explanation. The saddles (on left in photograph), loaned to the president by Ambassador Walter Annenberg, are fascinating. Each of the bronze miniature saddles represents a different type used in the American West. There were examples of a Spanish war saddle (1540), a mission vaquero saddle (1790), a Cheyenne Indian saddle (1820), a California ranchero saddle (1830), a Santa Fe/mountain man saddle (1840), a Mother Hubbard saddle (1875), a Great Plains stock saddle (1880), a Texas stock saddle (1885), a McClellan cavalry saddle (1885), a California stock saddle (1890), a women's sidesaddle (1895), and a swell fork stock saddle (1910). All were expertly crafted by Paul A. Rossi, former director of the Thomas Gilcrease Institute of American History and Art in Tulsa, Oklahoma.

Western themes dominated the art in Reagan's office. There were two sculptures by the contemporary artist Harry Jackson, one, the head of a cowboy, titled *Ol' Sabertooth* and the other called *Cowboy Meditation*. Senator Barry Goldwater gave Reagan

Common jelly beans appear colossal in the reduced Reagan Oval Office. Rex, Ronald and Nancy Reagan's dog, waits at the patio door. The King Charles spaniel was named after Rex Scouten, White House curator and former chief usher.

another sculpture, *Arizona Cowboy* (1899) by Ray Renfroe, and the president chose two Frederic Remington bronze sculptures: *The Rattlesnake* and *Bronco Buster*. He brought to the White House from California a favorite bronze he owned, *Smoking Up* by Charles M. Russell, depicting a drunken cowboy rearing his horse and firing his six-shooter in the air in the act of "smoking up" a cow town. The cowboy was the generic American hero, and President Reagan loved the qualities he was meant to represent: self-reliance and independence. The two other Charles M. Russell bronzes in the office were of bighorn sheep and western boxers.

Reagan chose to use the *Resolute* desk, the same desk used in the Oval Office by Presidents Kennedy, Carter, and Clinton.

George Herbert Walker Bush
Forty-first President
1989–93

It has been said that Frederic Remington's first sculpture, *Bronco Buster* (modeled 1895, cast c. 1903), was "the most popular . . . small American bronze sculpture of the nineteenth century." It stands 23 3/8 inches high. It is also a favorite in the twentieth century. The image of the cowboy and horse, like cast bronze, never tarnishes. Carter, Reagan, Bush, and Clinton have kept the sculpture in the Oval Office. The baby Remington, just under 2 inches high, is one of the few objects purchased for the White House replica and not made by John, Jan, and Jack Zweifel or their helpers.

According to Millie, the canine author, George Bush had a "secret" garden right outside the Oval Office. Millie naturally encouraged "The Prez" to work in the fresh air. Lying on her bed (see photograph) and being privy to high-powered discussions was not nearly as exciting as chasing squirrels and using the south lawn as a playground.

When the president did have to labor indoors, he worked at the walnut partner's desk he had used as vice-president. The Zweifels' miniature reproduction, standing 5 1/4 inches wide, 4 inches deep, and 2 1/2 inches high, is a meticulous copy. The desk chair is 3 1/4 inches tall.

The cane-back armchairs, placed next to the desk and around the room, were acquired in 1930 and have been used in the Oval Office since the Herbert Hoover administration. To make the copies of the chairs for the replica, eight tiny pieces of wood had to be fitted together to hold the nylon screen that gives the cane effect. Working on this scale requires the tiniest of tools. A drill bit of .016 is frequently used, but it is so thin it can hardly be seen. Staining the wood is almost as difficult as making the furniture; a drop of stain looks like a tidal wave when working on such tiny pieces. The cushion is made of bass wood, painted with a flat, water-based paint to give the appearance of upholstery. Oil paints are used to produce the shiny effect, as on the telephone, which has a light that really blinks.

The couches are made from a modeling compound called Sculpey. In the hands of a craftsperson, it can be made to look like folds in fabric or feather-filled pillows. The sculpting and painting of the replica's couches can take a trained artist a month to complete.

The Zweifels have made nine Oval Offices, and plan to make many more. For this reason, molds made of rubber, plaster, and fiberglass have been fabricated for most parts of the Oval Office, including the delicate moldings, wainscoting, pediments over the doors, and fluted seashell coves crowning built-in bookcases. The miniature replica of the marble mantel is also made from a mold. As in the original, the mantel consists of Ionic columns, and a frieze carved with drapery and rosettes. Over the mantel is the "porthole" portrait of George Washington by Rembrandt Peale.

William Jefferson Clinton
Forty-second President
1993-

The Oval Office is the command post of the presidency. On a typical day, it will be used for intelligence, national security, and staff briefings; meetings with dignitaries and visitors; conferences; and telephone calls. The president has a small private study adjacent to the Oval Office more conducive to reading, thinking, and taking a quick nap. President Clinton is generally at his desk by 9:00 A.M. and does not retire to the residence until 8:15 P.M. He normally gets about six, but would prefer, seven hours sleep.

During the day, the president may go to meetings in the Roosevelt Room or Cabinet Room, both close to the Oval Office, or walk to the Rose Garden or Old Executive Office Building (across a walkway) to make a presentation or offer a few remarks. Lunch is often served in the president's private study or, in fine weather, on the patio off the Oval Office.

Much of the furniture is permanent or semi-permanent, regardless of party politics. Every president since Kennedy has poked the fire with the same tools. The *Resolute* desk was used in the Oval Office by Kennedy, Carter, Reagan, and Clinton and used in other rooms by every president since Hayes except Johnson, Nixon, and Ford. What does change, often conclusively, is the art.

Clinton brought to the Oval Office his own busts of Thomas Jefferson, Abraham Lincoln, and Theodore and Franklin Roosevelt (and borrowed busts of

Ben Franklin and Harry Truman), to keep an eye on him (and vice versa). The Lincoln and FDR busts serve as bookends on the table behind Clinton's desk, holding, at one time, his copy of Vaclav Havel's letters written to his wife from prison, a biography of Robert Kennedy for which Clinton wrote the Introduction, and a Bible given to him by a minister friend. Also on the table sit a miniature of the bus he, Hillary, and the Gores traveled in across America after the Democratic convention (see page 194); a clay "Dad" made by Chelsea for Father's Day; a photograph of Mother Teresa; two small porcelain caricatures of Ben Franklin and Winston Churchill, both of whom Clinton greatly admires; and many family photographs.

On the east wall is the painting *The Avenue in the Rain* by Frederick Childe Hassam (1917). The red, white, and blue picture of flags flying along Fifth Avenue in New York is patriotic in feel and intent; it was made immediately after Germany announced that it would resume unrestricted submarine warfare and five weeks before America formally entered World War I.

Perhaps most revealing of all is Clinton's choice of Auguste Rodin's *The Thinker*, lent by the B. Gerald Cantor Collection. The president finds it a beautiful work of art that "shows the power of reflection . . . and because of the obvious enormous physical strength [of the figure], I like it because there is nothing weak associated with pondering, thinking and trying to work through something." But as no president wants to be deemed all reflection and no action, Clinton has kept Frederic Remington's *Bronco Buster* by his side as well.

The Clinton Oval Office was not complete in time for publication. The Zweifels had finished, however, the miniaturization of "The Thinker," two side chairs, and Socks, the "first" cat.

The White House at Christmas

A Gift to the People

Wouldn't it be nice if the President called you one day and said, 'C'mon over! It's your house! Enjoy.'

John Zweifel, *Los Angeles Herald Examiner*, November 6, 1979

This is something my children will never forget. That's what it's all about.

Exchange between a visitor to the White House replica and its creator, John Zweifel, Lufkin, Texas, November 1975

John Zweifel is pretending to tune a tiny television set with tweezers in this composite picture. Photograph of John Zweifel by Vince Eckersley, 1980. Photograph of David Letterman by Alan Singer; copyright © CBS, Inc., 1993. Photograph of Ted Koppel by Terry Ashe; copyright © Capital Cities/ABC, Inc., 1991.

John Zweifel wants to extend to every American a personal invitation to visit the White House. Not just to peek into the nine rooms roped off on the public tour, but to experience the entire building from East Wing to West Wing, from basement level to private quarters. He wants the landlords—the American people—to see and appreciate their house, the most famous house in the world.

Zweifel has aspired to show, through his creative skill, the architectural splendor and historic resonance of the White House. He has done it on a one-inch-to-one-foot scale. He argues that the White House is the best of all possible themes for a popular American display. But part of the long saga of the building of the replica includes the fact that practically no one, except his wife Jan, agreed with him at first. Only the Zweifels could visualize how a basically static model, what some people would call a glorified dollhouse, could delight and capture the imagination of millions of people.

The Zweifels instinctively recognized a number of factors:

1. *People are enormously curious about what the president's house looks like on the inside.*

2. *People respect the White House as a symbol of the country.*

3. *Most Americans would like to visit the real White House, but never have the opportunity to do so.*

4. *People want to see where famous rooms and gardens such as the Oval Office, Rose Garden, and East Room are located in the historic residential/executive complex.*

139

5. No matter how important the White House is, the average American can relate to it as a home with bedrooms and dining rooms and gardens.

6. Even in an age of short attention spans spawned by television, if people are given more than they can possibly see, fine craftsmanship and a few surprises such as working TVs and guards that occasionally turn their heads, they will be captivated.

7. People may not always understand or identify with "art," but almost everyone appreciates a beautiful, well-kept house and knows what it means to be house proud.

8. If the illusion is good enough, people will lose themselves in the visual experience and start thinking they are looking at the real thing.

Tens of millions of people (the Zweifels have estimated 43 million) have seen the White House replica, some of them having waited up to five hours at state fairs, convention centers, shopping malls, and museums. Random surveys show that only one or two out of every thousand people who have viewed the scale model have seen the real thing, and then, only the restricted and abbreviated official tour. The replica shows them so much more. The Zweifels were correct in believing a White House display would be popular and could succeed as a traveling exhibit. But there was a minefield between conception and execution. The making of an *exact* copy of the White House, a house where not only the president and first lady live, but where politics also resides, was not going to be without its trials.

In 1956, when John Zweifel was twenty, he took the public tour of the White House for the first time. He was enthralled, but even more curious than before. Only 5 rooms! That was all he was allowed to see out of the 132 he knew were there. Where did

Lincoln sign the Emancipation Proclamation? Which was FDR's Map Room? McKinley's War Room? Monroe's office? Grant's parlor? Where was Teddy Roosevelt's "new" West Wing? This was America's great house of history, the house that belonged to all the American people, and the public tour did not convey this sense.

Out of his wanting to not only know but also "see" more came the first glimmer of an idea to "do something" on the White House. Zweifel was then and still is a consummate showman, constantly thinking in terms of crowd pleasers. He carries in his wallet a quotation by the composer Richard Rodgers: "Nothing else matches the exhilaration of helping to conceive, plan and create something that has no purpose other than to give people pleasure." He is also a fabulous craftsman, able to make, as he says, "anything in any size."

John Zweifel has been whittling since the age of four. All through childhood and adolescence he collected Americana and crafted scenes of past popular entertainments, just for the fun of it. At sixteen, he started keeping files on the White House and, until he was eighteen, traveled during the summers with the Ringling Brothers circus. He delighted being on the road and setting up and taking down the endless equipment and paraphernalia. The sight of the crowd, awed by the spectacle in front of them, thrilled the young man. After moving elephants around, no undertaking seemed too difficult or unwieldy to at least contemplate. By the time he visited the real White House in 1956, he had already carved a 14,000-piece miniature replica of the 1913 Ringling Brothers and Barnum & Bailey circus and had been touring it for six years.

When Zweifel first started thinking about recreating rooms of the White House in the late 1950s, he fancied making them large enough for people to enter.

Simulated experience was common in theme parks and exhibition halls even before Disney. Zweifel was contemplating an exhibit in which people would be invited "into" the president's house. He wondered, though, should he transport them back in time or simply in space? What illusion was he after? Uncertain exactly the course to take, he nevertheless knew at an almost ridiculously young age that the White House was going to be the hook upon which his patriotic dreams were hung.

A self-declared flag-waving American, he fumed all during the civil rights movement, Vietnam, and Watergate that the White House was getting a bad rap. For Zweifel, the White House represented what was right, not wrong, in the country. Although he decided late in the 1950s to recreate the entire White House as a gift to the American people, that dream was only reinforced in the years that followed, as he became conscious of a desire to help heal the wounds of his country caused by ideological and political differences.

The White House is one of America's most pervasive symbols. The peaceful transition of executive authority in the world's oldest republic is exemplified by the change of occupancy in the house. The people decide who will be given the four-year lease, and if they don't like how the tenant behaves, they don't renew the contract. The only permanent resident is the democratic ideal. Each politician who occupies the building is only passing through.

The president of the United States lives in a house, not a palace, fortress, or castle. But oh, how that house is maligned. Sometime in America's two-hundred year history, the White House started to be blamed for practically everything its occupant did. Zweifel's strategy was to depoliticize the building. He decided to show the president's house out of context —away from the fierce in-fighting and odious maneu-

vering of Washington—and in a dollhouse scale. He was going to reproduce and reduce the White House and take it to the people. He became, in his own words, "a cheerleader" for the "grand old building."

Zweifel's most important early discovery was made in the Evanston Public Library: a large volume of detailed information about the 1948–52 Truman renovation of the White House with over fifty drawings, plans, and photographs. The volume didn't show the furnishings, but it did provide floor plans and dimensions.

One day, Zweifel realized, he would have to actually get into the White House and hoped that his good intentions would be enough to gain him entry. But no one at the White House was going to give him free access just because he asked nicely and said he loved his country. The metaphorical mountain he had to scale was higher and more treacherous than Everest; it was Washington bureaucracy. Patience was his most important asset on this uphill climb. He didn't have powerful connections in Washington. He didn't have friends at the White House. It was unlikely the president would call and invite him over.

• • •

John Zweifel was born in Monroe, Wisconsin, in 1936 and spent summers there until the age of eleven. They were part of the legendary Young family whose most famous member, and most radical, was the New York socialist cartoonist Art Young. Ray "Spot" Young, John's grandfather and Art Young's favorite nephew, was a flamboyant, well-loved Monroe character, a passionate entertainer and talented artist and woodcarver. Any thoughts Spot may have had about leaving Monroe for the big city as his uncle had, never materialized. His wife was adamant that the Youngs remain in Monroe and considered Uncle Art the worst of influences. Spot Young ran the gen-

Ray "Spot" Young in front of the movie theater in Monroe, Wisconsin, ca. 1939.

ist should be sentenced to life imprisonment, Art Young slept and even snored.

Heywood Broun, in the Introduction to the book *The Best of Art Young,* described Art's drawings as "the most shocking and scandalous cartoons, all done in the somewhat nostalgic manner of one who had been frightened by a woodcut in his early life. At a distance an Art Young drawing suggested the illustration for some moral maxim. Closer view revealed the fact that he was saying that every exploiter should fry eternally for his sins." (Later Broun wrote, "Here is a native son of this country who stems as directly from our own soil as did Gene Debs.") With a relative like Art, the Monroe Youngs felt they had to work doubly hard to prove themselves God-loving, patriotic citizens. As well as learning how to draw and wood carve while living in Monroe, John learned respect for the flag and the values of small-town America.

Family legend has it that Art Young was kicked out of the Coolidge White House for being impudent. Ironically, fifty years later, John Zweifel, his great-great-nephew, would have greater access to the home of the president than practically any other private citizen. For all their differences, passion, not financial reward, and an uncompromising spirit characterize the driving forces behind the accomplishments of Art Young and John Zweifel.

Both John's grandmother, with whom he lived when he was six and seven, and great-grandmother were often housebound. In order to share his experiences, he made three-dimensional models of the things he saw and did. He began to build a miniature circus so that he could show them the "wondrous Big Top" that his grandfather had taken him to see. Soon his grandmother was making the clothes for the circus performers that he and his grandfather carved.

John's father, Earl, started work as a sales repre-

eral store that had belonged to Art's father and from which the famous left-wing satirist had fled.

John Zweifel heard some stories about his illustrious relative while growing up, but mostly he was shielded from knowledge of the man who had been put on trial with three other editors of *The Masses,* charged with conspiring to obstruct the draft during World War I. The press reported that when the arguments were made in court as to whether the cartoon-

John Zweifel, age fourteen, with his miniature circus on display in his father's Ford showroom, Evanston, Illinois, 1950.

sentative for Ford, visiting dealerships around the country. He was sent to Detroit and eventually reported directly to Henry Ford II. After World War II, he quickly recognized that every ex-GI wanted a car, and he knew how to get them. So he left the company to set up his own Ford franchise on the north side of Chicago and became one of the largest car dealers in the Midwest, eventually owning fifteen franchises that sold new and used cars. He also established the sole Ford dealership in Cuba. It was during some of these

years, when his parents were working hard setting up their business, that John was looked after by his grandparents.

In the late forties, John's parents bought a large old house on Forest Avenue in Evanston and later a farm on the Illinois/Wisconsin border where they raised thoroughbred racehorses and had a herd of cows. John's older brother was sent to boarding school, leaving the younger Zweifel as the only child in the huge dwelling on Lake Michigan. This meant

John Zweifel with his miniature circus set up in the attic of his parents' Evanston, Illinois, home, 1952.

that John could store his collections in a dozen different rooms. Often the "precious objects" that he found cost nothing, only the promise to cart them away. There was always somewhere in the house he could store even junk and still have room to keep his works in progress set up and undisturbed. The attic was reserved for his hand-carved circus, which he had begun in his grandparents' home and to which he added new pieces weekly. (Today, the Zweifels own the finest private collection of circus memorabilia in the United States, including two of the most famous hand-carved turn-of-the-century circus bandwagons; wooden carousel horses; Barnum's notebooks, letters, and ledgers; and rare circus posters.)

By the time John was fourteen, he was taking his 12,000-piece, half-inch-to-the-foot "Greatest Little Show on Earth" on the road. His first venues were his father's car showrooms, with his mother or an employee driving him and his thousands of carved objects, many of them motorized and neatly packed in boxes, to Steel City Lincoln Mercury, Peoria Motors, and other locations. A headline from the 1950s read, "Zweifel's Circus Tiny, but Thrill Is Colossal." When John flicked the master switch, the lights went on, the calliope started to play, trapeze artists flew through the air, lions jumped through hoops, seals bounced balls on their noses, elephants took bows. The mini-midway was filled with hundreds of diminutive fun seekers. Behind the scenes, performers were dressing, the blacksmith was shoeing a horse, the cook was making flapjacks, and a policeman was deterring a small boy from sneaking under the tent. Inside these mini-performers were small gears, levers, springs, and hinges that had for the most part been the working mechanisms of manual typewriters.

At twenty, John registered at the Art Institute of Chicago to learn techniques and methods he could apply to the making of his exhibits. Unlike his fellow students, who he sometimes hired to work on projects back at his Evanston house, he never intended to become a fine artist. His love was for display and spectacle, but he had to learn painting, sculpting, drawing, and architectural design in order to create the ilusions necessary to make effective presentations. Of his Art Institute classmates, the one who came closest to his sense of fun and fanfare was Red Grooms; even so, the two men are worlds apart.

In 1959, a twenty-three-year-old John Zweifel married Jan Cleary, an interior decorator just beginning her career, and dropped out of the Art Institute before receiving his degree. He invited his circus friends—clowns, magicians, performers—to the wedding, but his future mother-in-law threatened to call the whole thing off if the elephants came. The Zweifels' honeymoon included setting up the miniature circus at the Circus World Museum in Baraboo, Wisconsin. John's grandmother, who had been making all the costumes "complete to the last piece of velvet, the last tiny sequin, the last button and buttonhole," for all the circus performers and workmen since John was six, was also there to help. The broadside read, "Stupendous Spectacular Pageants, mammoth menagerie, real Roman hippodrome, three ring circus supreme, 1000 people, 400 horses, gigantic street parade, rain or shine every show day." It was, as John was given to saying, "an overwhelming delight of amazement to young and old alike, ablaze with prismatic hues of circus colors."

Once the newlyweds got the "Greatest Little Show on Earth" up and running (it consisted of 40 electrical motors at this time, later to be increased to 130, and 36,000 pieces), with the fat lady, half girl, sword swallower, and the rest of the zany performers in place and the giddy crowds, carved circus wagons and full menagerie arranged, they visited a couple of real live circuses; at one particularly memorable mo-

ment, John coaxed Jan into a lion's cage. And of course they had to see firsthand the new Disneyland in Anaheim, California.

The honeymoon was no more unconventional than the next thirty-five years of their married life turned out to be. By the end of the trip, John was thinking about recreating "Great Moments in American History," a show that would feature Washington crossing the Delaware, the Wright brothers' first flight, Thomas Edison's laboratory, Barnum's biggest parade, the Boston Tea Party, the Gettysburg Address, and some significant event in White House history. He was prepared to start the enormous research involved. He also was considering building models of "rooms you always wanted to see": Liberace's music room, Hugh Hefner's bedroom, Julia Child's kitchen. John had already begun making a replica of the Gay Nineties *Cotton Blossom* showboat and its tug, the *Dixie Bell* (research and planning took seven years, construction three years), with showgirls doing the can-can, a paddlewheel that turned, an engine that moved, and a smokestack that belched smoke. In addition, he was determined to get his Chicago design business, Zweifel International, on a firm footing.

Earl Zweifel was a self-made man, savvy and successful in business. He did not support his son, either emotionally or financially, in what he viewed as a frivolous, if not downright juvenile, line of work. The junior Zweifel, too, became a self-made man, successful in the business that is also his pleasure. In 1959, he met with Walt Disney in Chicago for the first and only time and was invited to create exhibits for Disneyland. One of John's most famous Disney presentations was "Gardens of the World," sponsored by Ford. In 1961, Disney bestowed the honorary title "King of the Miniaturists" upon the young man.

In 1959, the average budget for a Christmas window in a large department store was $13,000, a huge

Jan and John Zweifel taking their two eldest sons, Jack and Jamie, to the store in the electric trolley John built, Evanston, Illinois, 1964.

In 1961, John and Jan bought a seven-bedroom home at 1027 Judson Avenue in Evanston, next door to Rand McNally and across the street from Oscar Meyer. Over the years, they filled the house with children, works in progress, and playthings. The latter tended to be John's. His basement had an old-time ice cream soda fountain with Coca-Cola (Zweifel's favorite drink) on tap, a hot dog machine, a regulation-size pool table with a parrot that shrieked "good shot" every time a ball dropped, and a theater, complete with proscenium stage, that seated one hundred. In the backyard was a popcorn wagon and part of a riverboat. John was the director of the Great American Trolley Company and kept one in his garage. He enjoyed taking Jan out for dinner in it.

The forty-foot living room in the Zweifels' house was always filled with exhibits. One was "County Fair," in which a horse race was activated by electronic tape so that even John didn't know which horse would win when they ran the course. There were suffragettes staging a protest, Dr. Killum inviting crowds to watch the medicine show, livestock wiggling in pens, children riding the Ferris wheel, a salesman cranking his car, firemen rushing to a barn to put out a fire, and Buffalo Bill and company performing their dazzling feats. From the outside, the Zweifels' house looked perfectly normal.

Zweifel was commissioned by Ford, Disney, and Fisher-Price to do displays for the 1964 New York World's Fair. In the 1960s and 1970s, he worked with Mattel, Disney, Fisher-Price, Ford, and the Chicago Museum of Science and Industry on special events and developing new concepts in toys. His father couldn't always believe businesses were willing to pay for the crazy, zany, fantastic things his son devised and devoted himself to, but they did, and they paid well. What no one would sponsor, because no one understood its "entertainment" value, was the Zweifels'

amount at the time. Stores allotted much more money for their "special events" budgets then than they do now, when most money goes into advertising. One year, John was asked to create Christmas displays for every major store window on State Street in downtown Chicago. For the Zweifels, starting in 1959, Christmas was 365 days a year. They kept their employees busy making fantasylands, country fairs, carnivals, rodeos, and medicine shows. During the Christmas season they employed as many as two hundred people part-time. John's imagination and know-how made up the dual fired engine that pulled this industry along. "Bunnyville" and "Candyland" delighted thousands of children at shopping centers and department stores across America.

supreme preoccupation, the White House replica.

In January 1961, the Kennedys took residence in the White House, and the whole country was enthralled by the glamour and life-style of the first couple. In that year, *National Geographic* came out with a special White House issue showing the White House in greater detail than ever before. There, on the pages of the magazine, was a two-dimensional scale drawing of how the White House looks in three dimensions. An artist and a cartographer had built a scale model of the White House and "liberated" each floor from its structural ties; they described their work as the "exploded concept" of understanding the White House. And the idea exploded in Zweifel's mind, too. There it was, the inspiration he needed to commence work on his own White House. He says he took the magazine to bed with him every night for a year.

Then came television triumph. Nearly one out of every three Americans watched "A Tour of the White House with Mrs. John F. Kennedy," aired on CBS in February 1962. Those involved with the broadcast later tried to explain the magic that transpired:

One woman talked and something profound emerged out of simplicity. The past stirred. Fact invited nuance; a hint became an overtone; a word summoned up an era. A frame of wood and a bit of cloth became a chair, and a chair summoned up a past President and a passage in American history . . . Not everyone was bewitched. But for some America stretched out, long and deep, behind the cultured lawns of the White House. Our sins, our excesses, our failures were there dimly, but our strength, goodness, and future were there too—outweighing our defects by far.

A woman spoke for an hour and the White House once more became the central symbol of America.[19]

Jacqueline Kennedy in front of the camera during the taping of the 1962 CBS television special "A Tour of the White House with Mrs. John F. Kennedy." Photograph courtesy CBS.

Now was the time, Zweifel concluded, with the White House in the historic consciousness of the nation, for him to make his move. In April 1962, he telephoned Pierre Salinger's office and spoke to an aide. He was referred to Pamela Turnure, Mrs. Kennedy's press secretary, and invited to meet with her in the East Wing. After flying to Washington and meeting with Turnure, he was told the White House would assist him in providing information and would also allow him to measure and photograph specific rooms. Security advised him on what he could and could not duplicate in a replica. The family quarters were off-limits, but the state rooms and a few others were to be made available to him. He was given his first "unforgettable" tour of the White House and its wings.

Zweifel flew back to Chicago heartened and immediately began work. He made drawings, using the floor plans in the book on the Truman renovation. He began framing the house and designed it to have a steel frame, wood body, formica skin, Virginia sandstone paint. This part alone would not be completed for eleven years.

On November 22, 1963, John F. Kennedy was shot and the White House sealed. The home became a fortress, impregnable to outsiders. There continued to be no special access for Zweifel at any time during the Johnson and Nixon administrations. He made requests for information but was told that even giving the dimensions of the piano was a security risk. He was shut out entirely except as a tourist on the public tour. And still, remarkably, he continued working on the White House throughout the 1960s and 1970s.

John and Jan and their six children, as they became old enough, started making the rooms of the White House, trying to glean enough details from photographs and reflections in mirrors in photographs to reproduce every chair, wall covering, drapery, ashtray, table, rug, and painting in every chamber. They also used sketches John made *after* the countless public tours he took, sometimes four tours a day. For these sketches, he relied on his memory and a system of measurement that involved knowing how many inches off the floor each of his shirt buttons was. He wrote to the White House. He wrote to every politician he could think of, asking them to help him gain entry into the White House to do research. Some elected officials tried to be of assistance, some didn't, and John now believes congressional pressure did him more harm than good in dealing with the executive branch. It became clear that the president's advisers were not going to have any senator or congressman tell them who should have special access to their boss's house.

John calls this time the period of "guesstation." Anyone else would call it the years of maximum frustration, as John continued to build the White House replica even knowing he was invariably making mistakes that would take hundreds of hours to correct. Every answer to every question he had could be found at 1600 Pennsylvania Avenue, but he wasn't allowed in.

While fighting intensified in Vietnam and Cambodia, while Nixon was visiting China and toasting Mao, while attorney general John Mitchell was leaving office to head the president's reelection campaign, John was asking the White House for measurements of furniture, the exact colors of fabric, and copies of paintings hanging in various rooms. The White House was not favorably disposed to this "pest" and, with controlled exasperation, answered most of his requests for information with either curt replies, token photographs, or nothing at all.

On March 20, 1972, a decade after he first was told he would have White House assistance in helping to make his replica a reality, John received a letter from the White House curator in reply to his latest request:

We regret to say that the scope of the material you require is beyond the feasibility of the White House staff to supply. Because we are not a research organization, we are unable to provide you with the extensive information you require. The only photographs of the interior of the President's House which are available for distribution are those published in The White House: An Historic Guide. *We are sending you a complimentary copy under separate cover. May we refer you to pages 96 and 97 which show a cutaway view of the White House?*

As we are certain you will understand, for security reasons, blueprints of the White House are not made available . . .

We regret that we cannot be of further assistance on this most interesting project.

John's reply of March 31, also written with controlled frustration, is characteristic Zweifel: earnest, naive, prodding, defensive, and rambling:

Thank you for your letter of March 20th. I was most disappointed with your lack of interest and support in my project. I hope you will reconsider your letter where you had regretted that you "cannot be of further assistance on this most interesting project."

I feel that you misunderstood my good intentions and am hoping that you will show me the courtesy of meeting with me immediately at your convenience. I would like an opportunity to meet with interested White House people and answer any questions they might have about this project or my experience. I am open for any ideas and suggestions. I feel the White House reproduction will be very educational, in an entertaining way, helping to promote greater interest and a better understanding in our American Heritage . . .

After that encouraging meeting [in 1962 during the Kennedy administration], I have worked for the last ten years on the considerable research and plans. In my present blueprints I have come up with a design that would meet the requirements that were suggested by the White House. Because of the definite support at that time, I took it for granted that the policy would always be the same.

This is the most exciting and challenging project I have ever tackled and its perpetual complexities are enormous. Without the cooperation of the White House, the model would not encompass the actuality and authenticity so necessary.

Thank you very much for sending me a complimentary copy of the White House: An Historic Guide. I had read and studied it many times but it does not answer most of the important questions about mea-

surements and colors that I have. Through the years I have collected much historical information and material on the Mansion, have files on each room, blueprints, large renderings and a small model for my research, all of which can be seen at any time. However, to assure exact detail, I still need access to better color material and measurements of all interior furnishings. This research can be done easily by myself, at your convenience. There will be many beautiful things made and then discarded because it did not meet with the highest of authentic perfection which must be met in this distinguished model . . .

There have been no definite plans made for the displaying of the miniature, but it is my dream that it will be ready for the 1976 [Bicentennial] Exhibition in Philadelphia. I would like to make the model reproduction a detailed record of the White House as it is today. With [your] simple cooperation, this miniature may become something unique and special for the sake of the generations to come.

There has never been any thought of commercializing this miniature labor of love reproduction; this is not the reason for doing it. My reasons are strictly honorable. As a patriotic citizen I am continuously trying to demonstrate my dedicated loyalty and devotion for the rich heritage of this historical monument and my country.

God bless the White House.

Yours truly,
John E. Zweifel

cc. C. Percy
    A. Stevenson
    W. Proxmire
    D. Rumsfeld
    R. Newman

It is too simple to say that no one in the White House knew if John was for real. They probably had never come upon anyone quite like him. What he was asking for was so strange. He actually wanted to know *everything* about certain rooms in the White House—the location of the light switches, the exact color of the wallpaper, the design of the fireplace, the shape of a chair leg, the pattern of the rug—and every other tiny bit of information he could get in order to make his model *exact* in every detail. At worst, he could be involved in sabotage. At best, he was a time-consuming constituent who didn't understand White House priorities. "Why doesn't he just go away?" many a White House staffer must have thought.

John decided to set a deadline, and the date would be 1976, the year of the bicentennial. Throughout his life, his targets have always been just a shade this side of impossible. In response to his letter, he received some photographs from the White House, and was given another private tour, from which he made sketches and notations, but what he really needed—measurements with which to make accurate blueprints and schematics, exact colors, and thousands of photographs of the interior and exterior—eluded him, no matter how nice or how desperate he sounded.

In 1973, the Zweifels moved to Orlando, Florida, as consultants to the major theme parks in the area. The following year, they hired the incomparable Roland Roberts, best known for his design of Cinderella's castle in Disney World and, prior to that, for his Hollywood set designs. In central Florida, the Zweifels were surrounded by some of the country's greatest craftspeople, many of whom were recently retired from Disney. Although Roberts had never worked with miniatures, he was brilliant with his hands and expert in the history of architecture. He worked for a decade for the Zweifels when he was

in his seventies and eighties. He made the staircase, the dining room pilasters, and the capitals on the columns on the north portico and in the East Room; he sculpted the mantels in the Red and Green Rooms and the candelabra in the State Dining Room; he molded clay and carved wood; and he created plaster casts and fiberglass molds and developed techniques for shaping Hydrocal, a kind of heavy plaster that can be carved.

Beginning in 1974, John and Jan, the five eldest children, Roland Roberts, other employees, and volunteers worked first on the frame of the house, then on redoing the Lincoln Bedroom (originally begun in 1963, 3 inches to the foot), on the Lincoln Sitting Room, and on the Treaty Room (again making many mistakes); they then carved the tiny wooden furniture for the Red, Green, Blue, East, and State Dining Rooms. The Zweifels moved forward by making the best of inadequate information and calling on personal finances, a lifetime of experience, careful calculations, and fortuitous guesses. They continued to work literally night and day on the White House regardless of the "It would be impossible for me to arrange to have photographs of the other wall taken for you" and "I regret to say that you seem to misunderstand our inability to be of assistance to you" letters arriving from the White House curatorial office. They persisted in requesting answers and photographs from the executive branch related to such specifics as the "top part of the ceiling chandelier," the shape of the "legs of the bed side tables," the "exact height of the ceiling," the "colors of the walls and the furniture."

The trauma of the Kennedy assassination, the quagmire that was Vietnam, Nixon's paranoia, all contributed to keep the Zweifels out of the White House and the staff unwilling and unable to answer the model makers' questions. White House duties did not include helping the Zweifels realize their replica, or as many in Washington called it, the "large doll-house." For solace, John saw the movie *Mr. Smith Goes to Washington* ten times. He attended the opening of *The Man of La Mancha*, and "The Impossible Dream" became his theme song.

Watergate was a watershed. In its aftermath, not only was Nixon out of the White House, but a new spirit of openness and trust was in. Zweifel was still writing to the curator's office, but now he was addressing his letters using curatorial assistants' first names. Staff people were friendlier but not any more forthcoming with the necessary information, and Zweifel was getting desperate. First, there was the replica to complete by July 4, 1976. Also, after long negotiations, John had met in Detroit on April 23, 1975, people from the Chevrolet division of General Motors, who were interested in supporting yet another of Zweifel's dreams: transporting the replica to all fifty states for the bicentennial celebration. The potential sponsor first wanted confirmation, however, that the Ford White House knew about the Zweifels' project and approved of it.

On April 24, 1975, the White House sent John what seemed to be a final "It is *impossible* for me to arrange" and "I feel that this office can be of no further service to you" letter. He was beside himself. He couldn't complete the replica without direct access to the actual rooms, and Chevrolet needed verification that the Zweifels had White House support, for which John had no documentation. The day he returned to Orlando from Detroit, April 25, John wrote to Donald Rumsfeld, whom he had known slightly in Chicago and who was now assistant to President Ford. What follows is the Zweifels' favorite story from the more than thirty years they've spent working on the replica.

On April 26, Zweifel telephoned the White House to explain the situation. He was told to contact Dr.

Cartoon dated August 10, 1974, by Tony Auth, *Philadelphia Inquirer.* Courtesy Tony Auth.

Theodore Marrs, special assistant to the president and public liaison officer. John telephoned Dr. Marrs' office, asked if he could bring samples of his work to Washington the next day, and was politely told that that day's schedule at the White House was completely full. Dr. Marrs suggested John send the material to his office and promised to look at it. On April 28, John nervously called his contacts at Chevrolet, who told him he had only one week to get the White House written approval.

John decided then he would sit on the doorstep of the White House if that was what was required. On the morning of April 29, he boarded a plane for Washington, arrived before 9:00 A.M., checked in to a hotel "for a week," and went over to the White House carrying a parcel containing miniature furniture and one complete room. The guard at the entrance of the Old Executive Building called Dr. Marrs, who got on the telephone and said, "Don't you know I told you not to come? It must be pretty damn important to you. Come upstairs."

Miniature Lincoln Bedroom furniture displayed in the actual room in the White House, July 1975.

When Zweifel, trembling, entered Dr. Marrs' office, the kindly gentleman asked, "What do you have?" John started to show him furniture from the Lincoln Bedroom, Treaty Room, and some state rooms.

"How did you do it?" Dr. Marrs inquired.

"From library books, guidebooks, magazine articles, photographs with reflections in mirrors, books about the Truman renovation, public tours," John answered.

Other White House staff came into Dr. Marrs' office during the meeting. By noon, Zweifel had seen the security department and had received security clearance. Dr. Marrs felt the miniature mansion *should* become a national bicentennial project. And for the first time in fourteen years, the White House staff were asking John how *they* could help.

By 4:00 P.M., John had telephoned Jan, telling her to quickly find a babysitter, pack up the rest of the Lincoln Bedroom and more furniture, and catch the first plane the next morning to Washington. "We are going to set it up for either the president or the first lady tomorrow. We will show it to the White House staff."

The Fish Room (now called the Roosevelt Room), a large conference room in the West Wing, was assigned to the Zweifels for their display. Security checked the tiny furniture for explosives. During the day, White House staff came in and out of the Fish Room, praising the craftsmanship and thrilled to see parts of the White House closed even to them, such as the famous Lincoln Bedroom and Jacqueline Kennedy's renovated Treaty Room. On May 1, John and

Jan were allowed on the second floor of the residence to set up *in* the Lincoln Bedroom the miniature Lincoln Bedroom and Treaty Room. There, President and Mrs. Ford saw the replica and were charmed.

John called the people at Chevrolet immediately to tell them he had obtained White House approval. But in the few intervening days, policy had changed at General Motors as to what the parent company and its subsidiaries should and should not do for the bicentennial celebration. Zweifel lost his sponsor. Dr. Marrs told the Zweifels that he would help them but he needed a little time, "as much time as it took to carve the rosewood table in the Lincoln Bedroom." He gave them the name of the appropriate official at the American Revolution Bicentennial Administration, ARBA, who was coordinating all "official" bicentennial projects. He then told them to go home to Orlando.

Letters were sent to American Motors, Ford, Eastman Kodak, Mobil Oil, Philip Morris, John Hancock, Prudential, Bell, Anheuser-Busch, STP, Studebaker, Xerox, Rockwell International, Bank Americard, Hallmark, Monsanto, Dow, Atlantic Richfield, RCA, US Steel, Borden, Colgate-Palmolive, Procter and Gamble, Union Carbide, and scores of other Fortune 500 companies asking for sponsorship or help. None wanted to be associated with even a "dollhouse" of the White House. For most, their excuse was that they were already sponsoring a bicentennial event and "current economic conditions" precluded other activities. These were early post-Watergate days, and White House references made corporate America queasy. "I just wanted a corporation to provide me with the materials so I wouldn't have to work 9 hours a day to support myself," Zweifel was quoted as saying in a Minneapolis newspaper, "and then come home and work another 8 or 12 hours on the White House."

Dr. Marrs suggested to John that he work with the White House Historical Society and through them

get ARBA recognition. Without ARBA, John knew he had no chance in convincing any company to put money into the White House replica. Eventually, after much letter writing and drafting of budgets and schedules, he would succeed in getting the ARBA seal of approval and a selection of fine tools from the Dremel Company, but no funds to support the fifty-state tour or the making of the exhibit. At every juncture, officials and bureaucrats questioned the Zweifels' motivations and methods. They never quite believed that a Florida family would spend hundreds of thousands of their own dollars and work like maniacs in order to create a "gift" for the American people on the two-hundredth birthday of the nation. In one letter to Dr. Marrs, John wrote: "Your friends in Washington are all so suspicious that I wish they would give me a lie detector test just to erase all doubts and then give me some support to do this right."

At the end of July 1975, the Zweifels received the first intimation that they might be able to do research at the White House while the Ford family vacationed in Vail. With only a few days' formal notice at the beginning of August, they were told to pack up their cameras and notebooks and come. John and Jan, pregnant with her sixth child, were joined by a student photographer, the only one they could afford, John's mother, and two associates, Gwen Dycus and Judy Berman.

The team had three weekends and two weeks to record the three floors. They brought with them lights, cameras, boards with 1-inch and 4-inch grids, tape lines, ladders, and lots of sketch pads. With the Treaty Room as their base camp and the historic 12-foot cabinet table (see page 154) at their disposal for making drawings, the team worked twelve to fourteen hours a day, in pairs, one person taking the measurements, the other noting them down. The State Dining

Unloading camera equipment near the north portico.

John, Kathryn, and Jan Zweifel; Gwen Dycus; and Wayne Blankenbecker seated at the historic cabinet table in the Treaty Room. They were given permission by the White House to use the table for drafting floor plans.

Room alone, with its intricate cornices, moldings, and woodwork, took four days to record. The housekeeper checked that each room was in perfect order before any photographs were taken. The only restriction was that pairs work in adjoining rooms or in adjacent areas so that White House security guards could more easily keep an eye on them. They covered the private quarters in the mornings and then came downstairs after the public tour was over at noon.

It was at this time that Rex Scouten, then chief usher and now White House curator, first entered the Zweifels' life. He helped facilitate their research that August and continues to help them more than any other individual at the White House. If the Zweifels hadn't dedicated the replica to the American people,

they probably would have dedicated it to him. He is godfather to the miniature White House.

The Zweifels returned home with all the information they needed. They had the colors, shapes, sizes, samples of material, and dimensions required to complete each miniaturized chair, sofa, carpet, painting, bedspread, drapery, ashtray, sculpture, stain, crack, doorknob, electrical outlet, floral arrangement, potted plant, wastepaper basket, window frame, table lamp, pillow, and personal effect of the first family. If they worked night and day, recruited enough volunteers, commandeered the children, hired staff, they would meet their first scheduled exhibition date.

The success of the replica depends on creating the illusion that the spectator is looking at the real

Wayne Blankenbecker holding on to John as he leans over the balustrade to photograph the cornice.

Researching, measuring, photographing, and recording the White House during August 1975. Photographs by Wayne Blankenbecker.

John and Jan noting architectural details of the house and wings.

John and Jan sketching the fountain and landscaping in the Jacqueline Kennedy Garden.

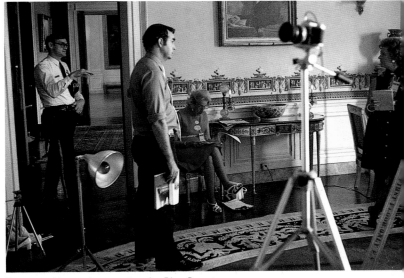

Photographing and measuring the Blue Room.

Jan studying the Library.

(Above) Gwen Dycus and Jan working in the Yellow Oval Room.

(Left) John and Wayne Blankenbecker measuring and counting the crystal drops on the chandelier in the Yellow Oval Room.

Jan working in President Ford's Oval Office.

Jan, seven months pregnant, next to the Chippendale highboy in the Map Room.

Jan, surrounded by vermeil, taking notes in the State Dining Room.

John and Jan in front of the Lincoln portrait, State Dining Room.

thing. Nothing can be out of proportion. No object, not even a light switch or table lamp, can be missing. Yet nothing can be placed in the replica that doesn't have a big brother in the actual White House. Lighting has to feel real and be varied. Exterior windows must have "daylight" or "moonlight" coming through. Shadows have to be precisely placed because the tiny bulbs don't have the power to create their own shadows, and sometimes shading must be dramatized to bring out details. Light bulbs in reading lamps burn brighter than those in chandeliers, and the chandeliers must have the illusion of hundreds of cut crystal beads.

In both the real and miniature White Houses, there are objects on every shelf. Books and flowers are everywhere. A visitor to the Zweifel exhibit will swear the chairs are covered with satin, silk, and velvet brocade, but the effect is achieved in many different ways. John says, "The textures of the couches, the fullness of the pillows, that is what makes the replica come alive." Whether wood is stained or painted depends on the size of grain and other factors. Whatever technique works to make each piece appear perfect is the technique employed.

John Zweifel has always maintained that the way to engage his audiences is to bring them up close to the exhibit, give them more than they can possibly see, and then put in some surprises. The desk in the Oval Office has to be there, but it is the pens, pads, personal items, and briefcase on the floor by the president's chair that overwhelm audiences. There is a fountain in the Jacqueline Kennedy Garden, but it is the water bubbling that enchants visitors. Pictures on the walls are important, but richly ornate frames help create the illusion of grandeur. All the elements are there to convince the public that the White House is residence, office, and museum in one.

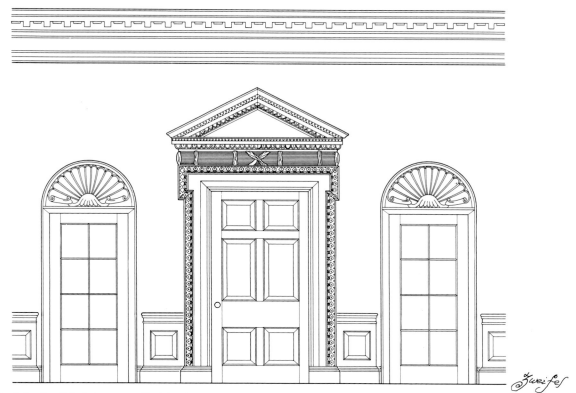

Scale drawing by John Zweifel of the east wall of the Oval Office showing the simple wainscoting, fluted seashell motif over windows, and carved pediment and decoration around the doorway leading to the Rose Garden. Zweifel made many such drawings before beginning to construct rooms.

The Zweifels estimated in 1975 that the replica would cost them over $1 million. Each room they assessed at between $20,000 and $35,000. They planned to book the White House replica in department stores, shopping malls, state fairs, museums, and conference centers throughout the country, many of which had displayed other Zweifel exhibits. There were never any plans to charge the public to see "their" White House. The hosting institution would pay between $3,000 and $6,000 a week, depending on the distance between locations and time of year. This revenue would go toward personnel, transportation, and maintenance and expansion of the exhibit. Part of the traveling display was a woodcarver's bench with someone, generally John or Jack Zweifel,

making miniature furniture and answering questions from the crowds. Jan made the bookings. There was no one to handle public relations.

The fifty-state tour commenced, with many rooms unfinished, in July 1975 in the Zweifels' hometown of Orlando, then moved to Tallahassee, Atlanta, and Savannah, Georgia. In November, an expanded replica was shown in Lufkin, Texas, where the entire town celebrated "White House Week." Every school in Lufkin taught the history of the White House, and every five minutes a different group filed past the house. From Lufkin, John trucked the replica to Biloxi, Mississippi. Finally came its debut in the nation's capital. The baby White House, whose gestation period had been fourteen years, was the spitting

Two views of the replica when it was set up on the Ellipse, Washington, DC, as part of the tree lighting ceremony, December 18, 1975.

image of its mother. During the annual Christmas tree lighting ceremony, it sat proudly but freezing on the grounds of the Ellipse, in the shadow of its parent. It then was moved to the Kennedy Center for the Performing Arts for eleven days.

Since 1975, the White House replica has been assembled and taken down nearly 300 times and has traveled over 200,000 miles in the continental United States. (The venues are listed on pages 195–201.) The replica is over 60 feet long and 20 feet wide. It weighs 10 tons. The table it sits on is 952 square feet. With the fence around it and two aisles, that area is increased to 2,590 square feet. It is packed in 40 crates every time it is moved, but that really does not describe the formidable task. A longtime volunteer, Robert Robinson, says, "The replica, when disman-

tled and surrounded by associate items, resembles nothing less than a giant puzzle impossible to reassemble."

The house itself is on wheels and glides smoothly in and out of its container, but every piece of furniture has to be individually wrapped in tissue and gently placed in the appropriate box. The furniture cannot be glued or fixed to the floor of the miniature rooms; it could not survive the bumps and potholes the truck traverses. There is always breakage after every move, but the object is to minimize the loss.

John travels with all the tools and materials he needs to repair any article, no matter how large or small. Along with everything one sees *in* the replica, there are also drills, paints, chisels, knives, sanders, electrical cords, light bulbs, dusters, window cleaners,

Q-tips, saws, cleaning fluids, lacquers, coils of wire, glues, tape, paintbrushes, fresh foliage, plain soil, bundles of wood, plastic and metal, and hundreds of other items used to maintain and repair the replica stored *underneath* the structure. The packing of these items is less problematic than making certain they are put in the same place every time so that whatever is needed can be instantly found.

In 1987, John Zweifel estimated that 22,000 volunteers had helped work on the replica. Most people can't find a half-dozen people to work for nothing. How does he do it? "I do it the same way," says Zweifel, "that Jack Mills did."

Jack Mills owned the Mills Brothers Circus. In 1942, as a young boy, John saw the circus and remembered how it was run. All across the country, there were organizations of circus buffs. Jack Mills would let it be known through this network when his circus was coming to town and that he needed volunteers. In exchange for a sandwich and a Coke, a free pass, and most important, an opportunity to go behind the scenes, Jack Mills got people to work an entire day, collecting tickets, ushering people to their seats, selling brochures. He proved that if you can find the people who have an interest in what you are doing, you can get volunteers.

When John signs a contract to bring the White House replica to a specific location, he requires that the site provide at least three or four people to help him unload on arrival and put the crates back on the truck at departure. Between those two times, John has the exclusive responsibility to set up, maintain, and dismantle the model.

Like Jack Mills, John knows who to call. Two of the organizations he usually contacts are the Chamber of Commerce and the Telephone Pioneers of America. The latter group, begun in 1911, is comprised of retired AT&T workers who had worked for the com-

Crowds viewing the replica in the Chesterfield Mall, St. Louis, Missouri, October 1, 1976. They did not know that after the prior showing at the Orland Park Mall in Illinois, the White House truck got stuck in mud and did not arrive in St. Louis until the night before the opening. Setting up the entire display overnight was a record.

pany fifteen years or more and numbers more than 820,000 members across the country. During his bicentennial fifty-state tour, John obtained so many volunteers through the AT&T network that he had to turn people down. They did everything from dusting to dismantling for a badge, a certificate, and the knowledge that they were participating in a patriotic, one-of-a-kind display.

John is obviously famous in the world of miniatures, and his White House replica has been given extensive press coverage in all the magazines that dollhouse enthusiasts read. Miniature groups, too, across the nation were contacted by John and Jan, and the volunteers that came forward from these groups made commitments to help from one day to

Trucking the White House replica across America from 1975 to 1980. John Zweifel has written: "The special White House truck has been from the George Washington Bridge to the Golden Gate Bridge; from the rim of the Grand Canyon to Alaskan glaciers; from Waikiki Beach to Daytona Beach. It has logged over 200,000 miles going to over 300 showings. It has been met by mayors with brass bands and shouting demonstrators. It has risked crossing striking truck drivers' picket lines and has been shot at. It has

ten years. They had the skills necessary to make wainscoting, repair furniture, paint walls, match colors, make petit point rugs, and generally do the work that needed to be done with tweezers, magnifiers, toothpicks, and a fraction of a single drop of glue.

Volunteers are ecstatic about helping with one of the most famous "dollhouses" in the world and certainly the most "American." Comments vary from "The most exciting thing I've done all year" to "I got to touch everything. I washed the windows with Q-tips" to "I actually climbed in and helped set up the East Room" to "I never knew they used volunteers for something like this." It is because of these thousands of volunteers that the White House replica is considered a "gift to the people, from the people." Miniaturists, because they know the difficulties of making such a house, have also provided some astute comments. One volunteer remarked, "Building the structure is wonderful, but creating the illusion is the

hardest. You have to fool the eye." Another spoke of John as being an "inspiration to anyone who wants to tackle an impossible task." Some marvel at the research, others at the handcarving of the furniture and the glass-blown chandeliers. All describe the replica as a spectacular achievement.

John speaks about the difficulty of holding an audience's attention. He says television has altered people's attention span and made it hard for them to know how to really look at and enjoy a visual experience. Most people, he despairs, are in a coma when looking at exhibits. He tries to wake them up, either by special effects such as the wag of a dog's tail or the wave of a flag or by a plethora of details too numerous for the eye to register. No matter how slowly the line moves, with people trying to peek into every nook and cranny, the Zweifel policy has always been to welcome them to the White House, tell them, "It is your house," and never hurry them along.

driven along all four United States borders. It lost its brakes in the mountains of Donner Pass, Nevada, and more frighteningly, going down a hill in Birmingham, Alabama, straight towards a loaded school bus. It slid into a cornfield during an ice storm in Kentucky.

Even through the hazards of traveling, thank the Lord the truck and exhibit are still in one piece."

John's intention on the fifty-state tour was not only to bring the White House to the people, but also to focus on the positive and unifying aspects of the office of president. To this end, walls were draped in red, white, and blue bunting, and patriotic music such as "The Ballad Hymn of the Republic" and traditional fife and drum songs emanated from a tape recorder under the north portico. Accompanying the replica were displays of presidential campaign buttons, souvenirs, and posters; historic photographs; flags from Kennedy's and Nixon's Oval Offices; presidential autographs; White House Christmas cards starting with Herbert Hoover's; and an actual White House dining room chair pulled up to a table on which were placed authentic examples of Eisenhower and Johnson White House china, menus from state dinners, and flatware and stemware of the same type as used in the State Dining Room.

The manager of a mall in Tucson, Arizona, wrote to the Zweifels: "The miniature White House is far more than a show-piece—it is a tremendous emotional experience. Witness the hundreds of viewers who took the time to speak with you personally in order to express their gratitude. I can think of nothing on the American scene today that does as much toward reawakening the old-fashioned Spirit of America, at a critical time [1976] in this Nation's history."

Jack, the Zweifels' eldest child, for years traveled with the replica, making innumerable objects, maintaining the exhibit, answering questions, and allowing people to watch him at his woodcarving bench. John always drove the tractor-trailer, which was painted red, white, and blue with WHITE HOUSE in big letters on the sides. For part of the tour, Rob and Margery Robinson also accompanied the exhibit. During this period in the 1970s, Rob drove the motor home and Margery drove the presidential limousine John had purchased at a government auction in Virginia. It,

Former Governor, now President Bill Clinton with John Zweifel at the opening of the exhibit in Little Rock, Arkansas, on May 29, 1979. Clinton, then only thirty-four years old, pointed to the replica of the White House and told Zweifel, "I'm going to live there." Clinton presented Zweifel with the Arkansas Traveler Award for his achievement.

too, was part of the political memorabilia that was displayed at every exhibition site.

After the arrival of the replica at a new destination, John, Jack, Rob, Margery, and the volunteers would work day and night to unpack, set everything straight, repair broken furniture, and give the house that "flower-fresh feel" that John demanded at every showing. In the morning, some of them, without having slept, would wash up in the motor home and prepare for the official opening ceremonies, ribbon cutting, and press conferences. John would don his red, white, and blue sports jacket and his Liberty Bell/ 1776–1976 tie and go before local television reporters, who always positioned themselves in front of the north portico. Their reports would invariably end, "This is ———, reporting from the White House."

Only the big, regional malls, with about a hundred stores, could afford to host the scale-model White House, and even then, they often took great convincing to do so. But after first insisting that they didn't show "dollhouses" or exhibits "without animation," that they were "not interested in history," and that "the White House can only be used on the Fourth of July," they would come around because of John Zweifel's reputation for providing spectacular entertainments. Even Neiman Marcus takes a Zweifel display.

In many areas, there was no local shopping mall, but the Chamber of Commerce, a civic group, and/or local merchants wanted to bring the White House to their area. They would find an armory or large garage, charge $3 admission, give John a third, and use the rest for local charities. State fairs were often the jolliest locations, with the model having its own tent or building, American flags flying, and the White House truck parked outside, functioning as a big billboard.

On the fifty-state tour, school groups and old people's homes were often the most enthusiastic. Rob Robinson was capable of talking for twelve hours a day. His wife would sell the brochures and some inexpensive books on the presidents and first ladies. There was little theft, although once, Rob's favorite object, the rocking chair in the Lincoln Bedroom, which he flicked whenever he passed it, was stolen. Early on, John put Plexiglas over the south front to prevent pilfering, but removed it shortly afterward because it came between the people and their experience of the house.

A week or ten days after the exhibit opened, John, Jack, and volunteers would start breaking down the exhibit into its five main sections and then pack the roof, the driveway, the north and south porticos, reference materials for each room, and the tools and supplies, simultaneously wrapping all the pieces of fragile

First Lady Rosalynn Carter and her daughter, Amy, observing Jack Zweifel at his woodcarver's bench, Union Station, Washington, DC, 1980. Jack, a ninth-generation artist, has worked on the replica his entire life. He speaks of the "endless hours" as worthwhile because of the "overwhelming response of the crowds" and the "wealth of experience" he has acquired during the years of being on the road with the miniature White House. Many of the replica's most finely crafted objects were made by Jack.

furniture individually and placing them in the designated plastic trays. Everything then was moved into the specially fitted truck. Night or day, when the packing was done, John would drive to the next venue, sometimes hundreds or even thousands of miles away. Two days and nights were needed to set the exhibit up again.

John confides that the route taken on the fifty-state tour was all wrong and that the schedule was grueling. But there was often no other way to reach the major state fairs and festivals across the country and to hit every state. The itinerary shows the replica zigzagging the nation. John was at the mercy of mall management. He often had little choice as to booking dates. Some years between 1975 and 1980, when the fifty-state tour was complete, he managed to come home only one day or one week per year.

In the summers, Jan and all six children would join John and travel together, living in the mobile home. They made furnishings, did general "housekeeping," and greeted the literally millions of visitors who came to view the home of the president.

John claims that his biggest headache while on the road was the weigh stations. "All you have to do is get one guy angry at the White House to have trouble," he says, and almost no one believed him when he said his eighteen-wheel tractor-trailer was noncommercial. "Nothing is noncommercial," was the frequent reply. Permits were needed every time state lines were crossed, which further aggravated the truck driver, who was really one of the country's foremost model makers.

Until 1992, John was the only one to drive the tractor-trailer. If there was a bump in the road, he wanted to be the one to hit it. His baby was inside. Since then, Gerald Matthess has transported the replica from East Coast to West Coast and back again. In Gerald, the Zweifels have found an individual of extraordinary skill, patience, and intelligence. He can solve any problem that arises and make anything that needs to be made. (In 1991, the replica had to be cut in half in order to fit into the exhibition space at the Ronald Reagan Presidential Library. John could manage this technically, but not emotionally. He entrusted the sawing and welding to Gerald.)

The press and public response to the White House replica has always been phenomenal. It regularly was covered the way John wanted the real White House to be: with favorable articles. The *Wichita Beacon,* under the headline "Crowds Flocking to See White House Replica," wrote: "It may be the biggest attraction to hit Wichita since Charles Lindbergh flew in more than 50 years ago." The paper quoted a source as saying: "The lines came the first day and haven't stopped . . . yesterday the wait was 4 or 5 hours for some people. We lost about 5,000 people who couldn't spend that much time waiting. We have been closing it off at 10 P.M. but it is 2 A.M. before we get the place cleared."

The Yorktown Merchants Association in Lombard, Illinois, reported an excess of 85,000 people visiting the exhibit during a twelve-day period, with 30,000 signing the registry and entering their almost unanimously glowing comments. In Crown Center, Missouri, 100,000 people came in eight days. Two fans in Terre Haute, Indiana, wrote: "You know, it really is our WHITE HOUSE and now that I've seen it, it seems more real to me and I feel like I'm really a part of it," and "Many people will never have the opportunity to go to D.C. to see the 'real White House,' but through your graciousness and generosity, they will at least know what it looks like." In Hawaii, where residents are most unlikely to see the real White House, commercial airlines and boat services brought schoolchildren from the various islands to Honolulu free of charge to see the mini-presidential mansion.

The White House Historical Association held a gala preview when the exhibit opened at the National Visitor Center at Union Station, Washington, D.C., in October 1980. It marked the conclusion of the fifty-state tour. More exciting still, Congress requested and President Carter proclaimed "American White House Replica Month" and urged "Federal, State, and local government agencies, interested groups and organizations and the people of the United States to observe [the month] . . . with appropriate programs, ceremonies, and activities." The White House replica is the only exhibit to have been shown in every state of the nation.

The replica continued traveling across America until 1982. Then, to celebrate two hundred years of friendly Dutch-American diplomatic relations, the government of the Netherlands invited the Zweifels to bring their "masterpiece" to Madurodam Park, located in The Hague and a famous showcase for miniatures. American Express sponsored the tour, and KLM flew the replica and the family over.

Published for the first time, a view of the damage resulting from the terrorist attack on the replica, Madurodam, Holland, 1982.

On Thursday, April 8, 1982, Queen Beatrix of the Netherlands opened the exhibit. Dutch newspapers carried articles and photographs of the monarch in front of the miniature White House in their "Style" or "Ladies" section in the back of the paper. After the opening celebrations and receptions, John, Jan, and the younger children returned to their hotel for the evening. Jack stayed behind to complete some work. Because he was staying late, security guards did not turn on the alarms in either of the two exhibition rooms. The mansion was in one room. The other room, containing the Oval Offices (which were a new addition to the exhibit) and presidential memorabilia, was where Jack worked throughout the early morning hours, music playing.

At 3:00 A.M. on Good Friday, just hours after the queen's departure, an anti-American terrorist group slipped into the room housing the White House miniature and attacked. With axes, paints, and solvents they attempted to destroy the "American White House." In twenty minutes, twenty years' work was ravaged and violated. The columns were smashed, paint covered the furniture, 435 of 480 handblown glass baby goblets were filled with paint and destroyed, 90 percent of the windows were broken, the wings collapsed under ax blows, the roof was drenched in paint remover and paint, 9 major rugs were ruined, 16 paintings were destroyed, 612 pieces of handmade pearlized silverware were mutilated, chandeliers were broken and their handblown shades covered in paint, walls were defaced, minuscule mementos such as the copies of Monroe's French centerpiece and John Adams' mantel plaque were smashed.

In Holland, John Zweifel's dream—that people would recognize the White House as a great symbol of America and lose themselves in the illusion he created, believing, for a little while, they were looking at the real thing—turned into a nightmare. The very

veracity of the model emboldened the terrorists, who perceived defiling the look-alike dollhouse as an attack on America itself. In the Dutch newspaper *Haagsche Courant*, the terrorist group Onkruit, which means "the weed," was quoted as saying, "Any festivity where the U.S. is concerned is out of place and should be fought with all measures. The White House should be destroyed, not praised. Any U.S. propaganda, no matter how small, must be countered." The director of Madurodam, Mr. Munck, spoke for the vast majority of the Dutch when he said: "We all stood there with tears in our eyes— when we saw it. It was so unexpected. You just don't think that there are idiots out there who would like to destroy a dollhouse because they don't agree with something."

John Zweifel, in the midst of this disaster, made a very wise decision. The replica did look just like the White House, especially in photographs. If he allowed pictures of the destruction to be released showing "El Salvador" written all over the north portico, the stately columns askew, anti-American slogans abounding, the name of the perpetrator looking like a billboard ad, he would have fulfilled Onkruit's intent. The boundary between what is real and what is make-believe would blur, and hundreds of thousands of people might imagine, even just for a moment, that a terrorist group really had attacked the American White House.

Leading magazines and newspapers offered thousands of dollars for the right to photograph the destruction, but Zweifel turned each one down. He issued statements such as "This work has nothing to do with politics. My wife, sons, and daughters and my mother only wanted to hold on to a part of history" and "You can't blame what maybe three or four or five people do on a whole country . . . [and because so many Dutch have responded so sympathetically] no wonder America has been friends with the Dutch for such a long time." He refused to show anger or act in any manner that might indicate his spirit had been broken.

The littlest Zweifels cried incessantly, and Jan feared for her family's safety. The queen issued a statement saying how brave the Zweifels were and that the American people should be proud of what they had done. She sent them gifts, but more important, had miniature specialists from the Royal Navy come and assist in the restoration. KLM flew volunteers and supplies over from the States. American Express paid food bills. Hilton Hotels put people up.

In the first fifteen days after the disaster, the Zweifels and friends worked 9,836 hours: 1,029 hours were spent repairing the exterior; 1,145 hours on the Red Room; 517 hours on the China Room; 1,663 hours on the State Dining Room; and on and on. It took a total of six weeks before the mansion

was again presentable and could, with Plexiglas covering the south side, be reopened to the public. The rest of the exhibit never closed.

Andreas van Agt, now an ambassador but in 1982 prime minister, remembers the Zweifels as "heroic." Ten years later, he recalled, "Confronted with the serious damage done to their splendid work of art, they did not lose their composure for a moment . . . the Queen of the Netherlands bestowed on John Zweifel a high decoration . . . to attest to her Majesty's and everyone's admiration and respect for the wisdom and dignity he showed after the disaster." The real White House, too, had faced near destruction when the British burned it in the War of 1812.

By July 14, just four months after the attack, the White House replica was presented to the British royal family at the Queen's Tournament in Earl's Court, London. In August, it was back, scarred and shaken, in the United States. As the replica toured back and forth across the country in the 1980s and early 1990s, repairs continued. The broken stemware and porcelain plates are currently being replaced.

The scale model went to the Minnesota State Fair in the summer of 1991. Robert Wherrett, who works as a jack-of-all-trades for the Zweifels, recalls that the crowds started gathering soon after 6:00 A.M. outside the building housing the replica, and the last visitors departed around midnight or 1:00 A.M. A tent was put up to shield the people in line from the sun, and drinking water was available. Periodically, medical help was required to treat those stricken by the heat. Regardless of the long wait and the temperature, it was a "must see" for Minnesotans. Why? Perhaps because the White House is central to the great American notion that any child can grow up to be president and live at 1600 Pennsylvania Avenue.

The White House replica appeals to every segment of society, crossing economic and demographic

Nancy Reagan giving California schoolchildren a guided tour of the White House miniature when it was on exhibit at the Ronald Reagan Presidential Library in 1992.

President George Bush viewing his office from a different perspective. Courtesy The White House.

lines, tickling the fancy of artists, craftspeople, home-makers, historians, veterans, and scholars. Ph.D. scientists find themselves as delighted as the children next to them in line. On the north side, there is architectural perfection: clean white lines. On the south side is a panoply of colors, lights, and objects. The senses are overwhelmed before a sense of history cuts in. The contrasts between the spare and the profuse, present and past, playful and serious, reality and illusion, make the White House replica an engaging entertainment and an uncommon instructive experience.

In the early 1990s, the White House replica began to receive institutional recognition. On November 4, 1991, it was the showpiece at the opening of the Ronald Reagan Presidential Library. It was seen by five presidents and six first ladies, a homecoming of sorts for individuals who, though their personalities and politics were varied, all shared the same bedroom at different times during the pinnacles of their careers. Nancy Reagan led schoolchildren on tours of the "White House," and Ronald Reagan reminisced in front of favorite rooms for the press. The lines to see

Barbara Bush attended the opening on December 23, 1989, of the exhibit "A Holiday at the White House" at Kaufmann's department store in Pittsburgh, Pennsylvania. The replica had to be hoisted eleven stories. A television crew filmed the White House miniature suspended from a crane, swaying in the winter wind, high over the city streets. Courtesy The White House.

The White House replica and model Oval Offices on exhibition at the Smithsonian Institution, 1992. Photograph by Eric Long, courtesy Smithsonian Institution.

the replica, decorated for Christmas, were up to five hours long.

John Zweifel always dreamed of seeing his White House installed at the Smithsonian Institution and hoped the institution would offer him a permanent space so that he could donate his White House to the nation. Only the first half of this lifetime aspiration has been fulfilled. From February 10 to October 14, 1992, the model was exhibited at the National Museum of American History, Smithsonian Institution. Over 4 1/2 million visitors came to the museum during that period, most of whom stopped in the room just to the right of the main entrance, where the replica was housed.

This period coincided, too, with the celebrations in Washington for the two-hundredth anniversary of the laying of the cornerstone of the White House on October 13, 1792. To further honor this historic day, John Zweifel had been asked two years previously to attempt a simulation of how the White House looked on March 14, 1797 (see pages 174–81). That was the day George Washington made his final visit to what would be one day be 1600 Pennsylvania Avenue but was then a busy construction site in a swampy, unpopulated, desolate region of the new nation. George Washington was pleased to see that the structure was not the palace that some had wanted, but a handsome and dignified stone house for the domestic comfort and public activities of the leader of the world's first modern democracy.

Unloading the replica at the Kennedy Library, November 1992. Visible in the photograph (but not once the display is assembled) is the steel beam across the center of the mansion; the door on the right, which is big enough for someone to go inside; and the Plexiglas ceilings of the rooms. All the rooms except the State Dining Room slide out like drawers. Each room has at least one box of furniture, seen here being unloaded from the truck. The six sections of the display are the West Wing, west colonnade, mansion, east colonnade, East Wing, and roof. Photograph by Alan Goodrich, courtesy John F. Kennedy Library.

Counseled by White House curator Rex Scouten and White House historian William Seale, Zweifel and his team of craftspeople built a 16-by-18-foot diorama at a ³/₄-inch-to-1-foot scale and displayed it in the lobby of the American Institute of Architects. Included were the scores of anonymous workmen who labored between 1792 and 1800 on the house: carpenters cutting their mortises and tenons and shaping the great timbers, whitewashers up on primitive scaffolding coating the raw stone, stonecutters dividing the large chunks with wire saws coated with water and sand, cooks, blacksmiths, teamsters leading oxen, wheelwrights. Also portrayed were Jeremiah Kale,

master brick mason, near his kilns and Collen Williamson, master stonemason, supervising the smoothing and carving of the sandstone.

Nothing in John and Jan Zweifel's long career excited them more than being asked to set up the "Building of the President's House" in the White House itself. The Zweifels moved their recreation into the East Room, right under the eyes of George and Martha Washington and below the Bushes' sleeping grandchildren, on the night of October 13, 1992. Over the next four days, President and Mrs. Bush, dignitaries, and the public got to view this amazing reenactment as part of the celebrations for the two-

Sharon Coyne (center), who made most of the figures for the display "Building the President's House," and John Zweifel (left), showing Rex Scouten (right), White House curator, their progress, January 1992.

hundredth anniversary of the White House.

The White House replica departed the Smithsonian Institution for the John F. Kennedy Presidential Library at this time. It remained in Boston until popular demand brought it back to the Ronald Reagan Presidential Library in Simi Valley, California, in the fall of 1993. The miniature White House then traveled to Tokyo as part of the large American Festival Japan '94, organized by the Smithsonian Institution, the Japanese government, and a group of Japanese sponsors.

In a letter written on May 11, 1993, President Clinton described some of the objectives of this festival.

The American Festival Japan '94 offers a wonderful opportunity for the people of the United States and Japan to strengthen our friendship through direct communication and educational exchange. The Smithsonian Institution's unprecedented exhibition of American history and culture will offer Japanese audiences a chance to experience America and our people as we see ourselves. The Japanese people will have a chance to share in the enjoyment of some of our most precious historic treasures, such as the Wright Brothers airplane and relics of the Old West, as well as our most cherished forms of entertainment . . .

. . . Events such as the America Japan Festival '94 are helping to increase international communication and promote deeper appreciation of each nation's cultural heritage.

The Zweifel family have devoted their lives to underlining the importance of the White House as part of America's cultural heritage. Now, because they had the foresight to make the White House portable, it serves as an ambassador-at-large.

William Seale, White House historian, was asked by this author for his opinion concerning the Zweifels' American masterpiece:

One leaves the replica with a deeper understanding of the character of the use of the White House as well as a fuller idea of the building itself. A view with such scope could not be obtained even from a plane! This is a sort of visual education that draws the viewer closer to the subject . . . I will say that after studying the White House for years, I learn something new every time I see the miniature replica . . .

Anyone who brings together a mass of facts this way and interprets them has accomplished something very fine. Mr. Zweifel has a genius for detail—there is not a blank spot, no blind TV's, no bare tabletops. How does he do it, one asks?

The Zweifel family with President Reagan during a special showing in Orlando, Florida, September 27, 1990. From left to right: Jack, Randy, Janet, John, President Reagan, Jan, Helen Cleary (Jan's mother), Julie, and James.

[It is popular] because anyone can relate to it . . . Miniaturization carried out with this level of skill has an Everyman appeal. And isn't this the ultimate Everyman house? The White House, residence and workplace of the President of the United States, is our closest point of human contact and identification with a vastly complex governmental system.

The White House is shorthand for the presidency itself; it speaks to all, more than the Eagle, more than Uncle Sam, because it is an essay, not a sign.

As the White House changes, so, too, the replica. As the Clintons redecorate, so, too, will the Zweifels. The flow of first families means the house will never rest in state. It is, as Seale says, "an essay, not a sign." Some child, living today above or below the poverty line, from any one of a hundred ethnic or cultural backgrounds, will grow up to live in the big white house on Pennsylvania Avenue and be the leader of the strongest nation on earth. It is a terrific story. The White House helps us look back with pride on our nation's past and requires us to face, with hope, our country's future.

The Building of the President's House

"The building of the President's House," a 3/4-inch-to-1-foot scale model, 14 by 28 feet, of the White House as visualized on March 14, 1797, the last time George Washington visited the construction site. Photographs taken on location at the American Institute of Architects, Washington, DC.

In the foreground are brickmakers mixing clay and pressing it into blocks, bricks ready for firing in the kilns (seen on the left and right of the photograph), and piles of fired bricks. In the distance are carpenters cutting and shaping planks of wood, workmen using a pulley system to lift materials to the second floor of the house and the roof, a master stonecarver working over the north entrance, and painters applying whitewash.

Constructing the basement groin vaulting using a specially fabricated wooden frame. The magnificent brick arches in the basement (or ground) level were once hidden from the public when they were part of the maintenance and housekeeping areas, but are now a striking architectural element seen by visitors when they first enter the mansion. The brick, made on the construction site, remains in the White House today, having survived the burning by the British in 1814 and the gutting of the White House during the Truman renovation 1949–1952. The brick lining the walls is two feet deep and during the renovation the walls were reinforced with concrete underpinnings and a steel frame.

The Aquia Creek sandstone was brought to the building site by boat from the quarry downriver, dragged from the Potomac by oxen, and then cut. Wire saws, doused with water and sand, were used to cut the stone. The blurred man sharpening tools is one of a number of motorized figures that capture the viewers' attention.

The fenced stoneyard, where every cut stone has already been given a number, is in the center of the photograph. The master stonemasons and stonecarvers, most of whom came from Edinburgh, Scotland, laid the cornerstone on October 13, 1792, and continued to work from mid-April to mid-October every year until John Adams occupied the house in 1800. The White House stone carving is considered the finest in the United States.

(Left) The original three floors of the house are clearly depicted. The top of the brick groin vaulting is the bottom of the first (or state) floor. In the photograph, workmen are laying a wood floor on it. On the second story, a room is being framed.

Virginia sandstone is highly porous and needs to be sealed upon placement. The whitewash, applied to the house like paint, was an unusual combination of ground limestone, salt, ground rice, and glue. In 1980, work commenced to remove more than thirty coats of paint that had been applied since the original whitewash, some of which was still sticking to the stone in the 1990s. Workers mixing the original whitewash are in the center of the photograph.

This photograph shows the north side of the house, from a point approximating what is today known as Lafayette Park; Pennsylvania Avenue being just above the horse's head. James Hoban, the architect, points to his masterpiece while showing President Washington the workmen's progress. Washington was honored with a 16-gun salute.

Technical Appendix

The following is a very partial answer to the frequently asked question of how the Zweifels did it. The Zweifel family would like readers to realize that each part of the replica presents its own challenges, and there are no fixed or final solutions. They use any technique that works, each technique having been acquired through trial and error.

Adhesives

As a young man, John Zweifel was called in to help repair miniature furniture in the famous Thorne Rooms at the Art Institute of Chicago. Because so many of the problems were a result of adhesives drying out, John describes himself as a "glue freak," always looking for a stronger and clearer glue. He uses, among others, Elmers glue, which dries clear; super glues; super epoxies; and clothes pins as clamps.

Animation

Smoke comes out of the chimney from a steamer (the same kind used by dry cleaners) underneath the replica. Working TVs are handheld models (originally, John Zweifel had used full-size units whose images were reduced through a system of mirrors and lenses). The guards in front of the Map Room, in the guard house, and behind the window in the Blue Room at Christmas move by a system of small, internal levers run by motors under the replica. A regular watch face keeps correct time in the tiny grandfather clock. A recirculating pump underneath the replica pushes water up the pipe that forms the spout of the fountain in the Jacqueline Kennedy garden. Tape recorders equipped with endless tapes make the telephones in the Oval Office and the Library ring intermittently. A fan pushes air around the top of the replica to cause the flag to flutter. Light switches in the President's Study turn the lights in the room on and off. The fire effect in fireplaces is created by a staggered current and microchips that make the fire blink. A VCR and mirror below the Movie Theater produces a video rear projection on the screen. Additional animation currently being developed includes steam coming out of the kettle in the kitchen and clouds moving across the ceiling.

In the Blue Room Christmas scene, the falling snow effect is produced by a recirculating fan creating a vacuum that sucks the styrofoam "snow" to one end and then throws it out again; there is a whiff of pine; the trees bend slightly back and forth; "icicles" form; a guard shivers; cold air blows out at those looking in; and Christmas music plays. Newly added (and not in the photograph), a tiny train on an N-gauge track goes round and round the tree.

Candles

Formed candle wax; tubes with electric micro flame bulbs; simple toothpicks shaped and painted.

Carpets

see Rugs

Chandeliers

To copy and reduce a complex lighting fixture, photographs are taken of the original from every possible angle and then photocopied to scale. Drawings are made and studied, and blueprints are produced.

Tubing and metal are shaped by hand and soldered; brass rings and finished washers are frequently used. The crystal effect comes from strung beads and hand-blown glass; if too much glue is used, beads do not hang correctly. Glassblowers are commissioned

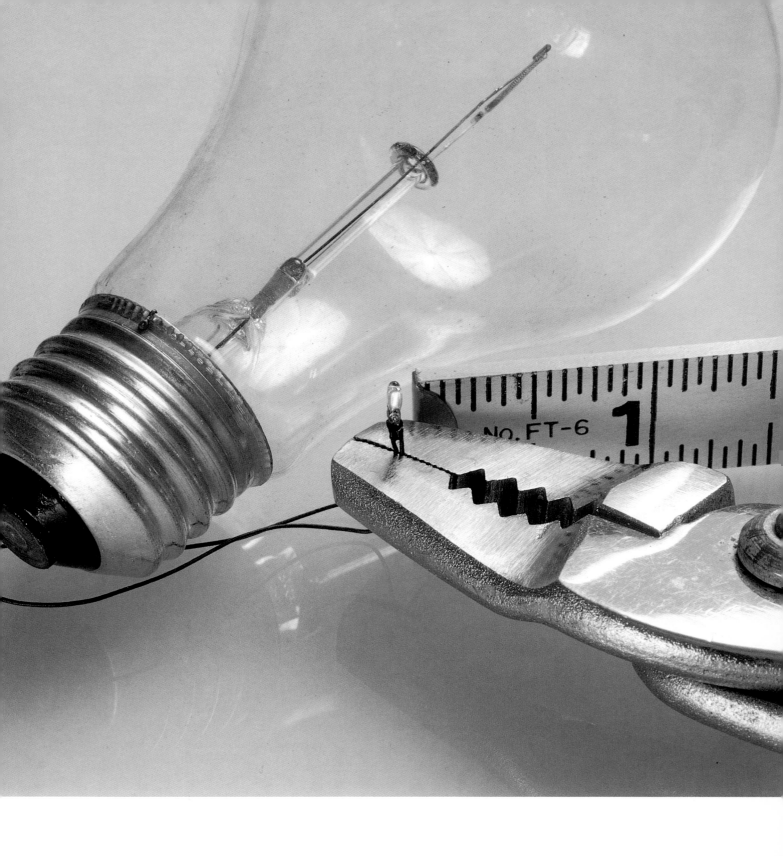

John and Jan with expert carpenter Leon Bartkowiak, working on the framing of the house and the plywood skin. After outgrowing their living room and garage, the Zweifels rented a large Orlando, Florida, warehouse, a former cannery, vacated by Disney. Top photograph showing the south side and bottom photograph showing the north side were both taken in 1974.

depending on their specialty—i.e., straws, ribbons, crystal arms, shades, etc. (The East Room chandeliers are blown in one piece at a cost of $10,000 for the three; each chandelier contains 55 tiny light bulbs, each with two wires.)

Chandeliers are taken out every time the replica is moved; each move necessitates snaking two super-thin wires up through the ceiling of the room and the interior of the house to the transformer that regulates the intensity of that particular fixture; it takes approximately four hours to change one light bulb in a chandelier.

Curtains and bedspreads
Normally, fabric is glued over carved wood, so that every pleat stays in place and in proportion; each fringe and tassel is knotted separately.

Electricity
The display has 6–8 separate 110-volt circuits with about 50 variable transformers—twice that many when decorated for Christmas. The main power comes in from the source, runs into a full-size circuit breaker, then goes to six regular power strips, to double-fused strips with 12 or 16 outlets, and into another strip of outlets triple fused. John Zweifel calls this a "balancing act of power." Each of the five sections of the exhibit is separately fused and each has its own fire detector.

Exterior of mansion
The exterior is a steel frame, a wood body, a formica skin (which covers unsightly screw heads, seams, and imperfections in wood), and white Virginia sandstone paint. In 1991 the mansion was taken to a welder's shop and cut in half so that it could fit in the doorway of the Ronald Reagan Presidential Library; the frame was refitted with an I beam (cost of cutting, $15,000).

Fabric

Often silk screen or paint directly on wood. Creating the correct *illusion* of depth, color, texture, finish, and style is the ultimate criterion for what technique to use; this can take days of testing to arrive at. The use of actual fabric would generally result in the improper scale.

Finishing work

Every surface requires the right texture and feel. The exhibit travels with ten finishing sprays, including dulling, matte, weathering, satin, pearl (looks like silk), gloss, crystal clear; different fixatives and preservatives such as Scotch Guard (finishing sprays change the color of fabrics and paints and must be accounted for when choosing the initial colors); over fifty colors each of flat and gloss paints; fifteen different inks; and twenty-five kinds of stain.

Flags

Carved out of wood or sculpted out of modeling compound and then painted; sometimes made of fabric.

Floors (parquet)

The floors are often walnut and oak or mahogany and bass. Every strip needs to be cut by hand perfect-ly so that it butts the adjoining strip. After the floor is laid, a high-gloss finish is carefully poured over it (one coat equals 50 coats of varnish). An Oval Office floor takes approximately 200 hours to fabricate (see right).

Floors (regular)

Start with a flat surface, cut tiny boards to scale, sand the edges, stain them to the proper color, fit them tight to look like tongue and groove, glue the boards down, and cut to fit the size and shape of the room.

Flowers and fruit

Most of the miniature arrangements are made by artist and gardener Barbara Meyers of Chicago. She studies flowers in her garden or, when the ones she needs are not blooming, looks at gardening catalogues. Her arrangements are based on photographs of White House floral arrangements. They were originally made out of bread dough but mice ate them; now they are made out of Sculpey compound. Meyers works with fingers and toothpicks; each rose petal is made separately and assembled with white glue; lilies are made from a teardrop shape and assembled. Flowers, fruit, and leaves are painted with acrylic paints. As in the real White House, the miniature floral and fruit centerpieces are larger in scale than expected.

Flower pots

Thimbles; toothpaste lids; clay for terra-cotta; carved wood; blown glass; cast pewter; and disposable plastic and paper creamers such as used in restaurants and cafeterias (these also function as lampshades). They are often painted and/or finished with 14K gold and silver plate.

The bed has been used in one room or another in the White House since 1861. It originally had "Pattent [sic] Spring Mattresses," newly invented and highly prized. Willie Lincoln died in this bed in 1862; Abraham Lincoln was embalmed at the foot of it in 1865. Grover Cleveland's daughter Esther was born in the bed; Woodrow Wilson recuperated from his stroke in it.

Lincoln thought it was inappropriate that his wife should have purchased this elaborate, expensive piece of furniture, almost 9 feet long by 6 feet wide, when Union soldiers did not have blankets to keep them warm. A simpler bed at such a serious time was more in line with Lincoln's convictions. Yet this bed, fit for a king, carries the name of the man who was born in a log cabin and remembered for his simple ways.

Fret work

The original is carved wood. If it is longer than 3 feet, a mold is made out of plaster or fiberglass and plaster is then cast in the mold.

Furniture

Originally the White House replica was called "The Hand-Carved White House in Miniature"; all the furniture was carved in wood and, whenever possible, the same wood as the actual piece of furniture in the White House was used; now certain pieces are sculpted from compounds such as Fimo or Sculpey. When more than 30 of the same type of chair are needed (i.e., Blue Room, State Dining Room, Cabinet Room) the first is carved out of wood and the rest are cast pewter; the furniture is then painted and finished (see "Finishing Work").

Hardware

The workshop for the replica is stocked with different sizes of tubing, nails, pins, screws, wire, and metal; these are pounded and shaped to make hinges, doorknobs, and locks (some doorknobs are also made from jewelry beads).

Landscaping

Grass is made from dyed-green sawdust, dried moss, lichen, and ready-made plastic particles. Trees are formed by soldering wire to form branches which are then covered with a sculpting compound called Bondo. Leaves are made from shredded pieces of fabric and leather which are cut and painted, or ready-made plastic leaves. The leaves are glued on individually; during autumn months, specially prepared red and yellow leaves are strewn on the replica base; potting soil is used for soil; moss is used in flower beds; and topiary are built of plastic leaves.

Lightbulbs

There are about thirty styles of miniature lightbulbs, including screw-in bulbs; most are the size of a grain of rice (see page 183). Most of the circuit boards are imported from Europe; transformers regulate the light intensity—i.e., a 12-volt bulb may be run at 3 volts to simulate candlelight, 6 volts in wall sconces, and full voltage in table lamps or divided among the many bulbs in chandeliers; fluorescent lightbulbs are used in the Cabinet Room and the Press Room.

Lighting

The ambience of the display comes from the lighting; every room has different lighting contrasts and intensities; light fixtures in the rooms are for effect, not true illumination. The ceilings are of opaque white Plexiglas that allows light from ordinary spotlights to come in from above; the Oval Offices have indirect lighting around the dome; and the north portico is lit with spotlights hidden behind the gate piers. The entire display is normally illuminated with ceiling spotlights provided by the exhibition site.

Mantels

Carved from wood with a few areas made of Hydrocal, which is easier to work with in small areas.

Marbleizing

Various techniques are used, including application of paints and inks with small sponges, small feathers, steel wool, rope strands, toothbrushes, Q-tips, pins, human hair, and very fine brushes and pens.

Outdoor furniture

Pieces are made of wire and a small amount of fiberglass; if multiple copies are needed, a fiberglass mold is made.

Picture frames

Carved or built up from thin strips of wood, sometimes milled specially, sometimes store-bought molding; each miniature frame matches a specific one in the White House.

Rugs

The finest ones are petit point. Some are initially painted on fabric or oil cloth until final petit-point rugs are ready.

The half-finished petite petit-point rug took miniaturist Judith B. Ohanian "hundreds and hundreds of hours of work." Started in the mid-1980s, it was still not complete in the mid-1990s when the antique rug in the Blue Room upon which it was based was designated irreparable and in need of replacement. The miniature rug, never to receive the wear and tear of the original, was nevertheless obsolete.

Making the chart, seen in the bottom of the photograph, took as long as the needlework. The rug was made on imported Swiss gauze, 30 stitches to the inch or 900 stitches to the square inch. The six-stranded cotton floss was imported from France, three strands only per stitch. A #26 tapestry needle was used.

Judith Ohanian cannot even estimate how many more "hundreds of hours" would be needed to complete the rug. When she stopped stitching, she had not even begun to draw the ten *different*, "enormously complicated" charts needed for the intricate border which changes with each angle of the curve.

Stemware

Professional glass blowers took 3 ½ months to make the 480 wine, water, and champagne glasses for the State Dining Room. 435 were destroyed in the terrorist attack in Holland; they were replaced temporarily with plastic glasses. (Also needing to be replaced were 612 miniaturized pieces of pearlized flatware and 120 hand-painted porcelain plates destroyed in the attack.)

Tools

The most important tool is a good knife for woodcarving; surgical and dental tools are excellent for working on a small scale (knives, blades, tweezers, scissors, sutures, scalpels, and mirrors for seeing around corners); Exacto knives (Exacto was a sponsor of the exhibit in 1976); Dremel tools (Dremel donated thousands of dollars' worth of tools), including a moto-tool kit with grinders, drill bits (.016 is the smallest), drum sanders, cutters, router bits, and speed scroll saws (see photograph opposite). Also needed are table saws and jigsaws, small clamps, magnifying glasses, pencil-point soldering guns, precision airbrushes, a lathe, and specially designed tools and jigs.

Wainscoting and dentils

As many as fourteen pieces of wood molding are built up to make one piece.

Wood

When possible, the same wood as the furniture being copied is used. Frequently used woods are mahogany, cherry, and rosewood. Orange crates serve when the kind of wood either doesn't show or doesn't matter.

Wood stain

Twenty-five different wood stains and tinted denatured alcohol are used; it is difficult to get an even stain over small surfaces without puddles forming in the corners. The grain is often painted by hand using calligraphy pen tips and india ink.

Rooms in Progress
Carpenters' Shop

A miniaturized detail of a corner of the basement carpenter's shop. The gold chairs, selected for the White House by Mrs. Kennedy, are constantly in use and frequently in need of repair. President Johnson described them as "toys." The White House carpenters recently made the bookcases in President Clinton's office in the residence.

Kitchen

Pots, pans, vegetables, trays of cookies, and assorted hors d'oeuvres—part of the miniature kitchen modeled upon the original located under the family dining room. In 1991, 34,526 people were served food in the White House, all of which was prepared on the premises.

Photographer's Note

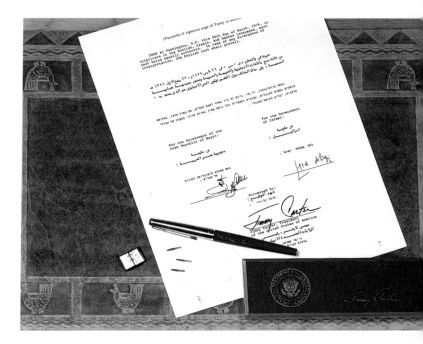

The following were the greatest challenges to photographing the miniature White House:

Dust
Dust appears to be the size of meteors inside a miniature set. When possible, the area must be cleaned with antistatic chemicals. Slow movements are imperative so as not to stir up additional dust. During long exposures, dust might actually land and ruin the shot.

Lighting
Lighting a miniature set is difficult because bright lights produce unlikely shadows or make the scene appear unnatural. Credibility depends on precise and exact lighting. Each view needed its own special attention. Both strobe lighting and tungsten lamps were employed as needed.

Space
Reaching into a miniature set with a full-size light meter can easily result in furniture crashing and flower arrangements toppling. Extreme care is required. Getting a large-format camera in close enough for the shot is always difficult, sometimes impossible.

Electricity
It is necessary to have a stable electrical current. Fluctuation in the electrical output affects color. Blown circuits present obvious problems. Knowing what the equipment can handle is essential. On-site electricians are helpful and are consulted.

Time
The average length of time to set up and make each photograph in the book was approximately $3\frac{1}{2}$ hours. Some took as long as 7 hours to make. Exposure times ranged from $\frac{1}{15}$th second to 30 minutes.

Preparing the miniature room (finding and fixing slight imperfections, dusting, etc.), moving the camera and tripod into position, setting up lights, calculating exposure times, doing Polaroid tests, making four exposures of each composition, is *extremely* time-consuming. Vibration, however slight, may ruin an exposure.

Arrangements
In photographing normal miniature rooms, the photographer has a great deal of latitude in arranging the furniture and other objects so that one item does not obscure another in the final photograph. A prerequisite of photographing the miniature White House was that the furniture must be in the same position as in the real house. Only the slightest adjustments were permitted.

The finest quality cameras and lenses were employed in the photographing of the miniature White House. These include a 35mm Nikon, a $2\frac{1}{4}$ Hasselblad and a 4 x 5 Sinar F and 55 macro, 80mm, 90mm, 135mm, 210mm, and 350mm lenses. Many film types were used, depending on the situation.

"That bus really did carry us to the White House," stated President Clinton during an interview with C-Span in the Oval Office. When he, his wife, and the Gores got on the bus right after the Democratic convention in the summer of 1992, it connected them directly to the American people. The bus reminds Clinton of his pledge to change America for the better and he keeps it always behind his desk in the Oval Office as a reminder of his promise.

The photograph is reproduced lifesize. Zweifel's tiny bus is part of the miniature replica of Clinton's Oval Office.

Itinerary: Fifty State Tour

The replica has criss-crossed the country numerous times and visited every state in the nation at least once. It has also traveled to Holland, Britain, and Japan. In 1975, John and Jan Zweifel announced, "We're taking the White House to the people." The following itinerary illuminates their unprecedented achievement.

Alabama

1976
Dothan: Northside Mall
Jan. 27–Feb. 11

1979
Mobile: Springdale Mall
May 8–19

1981
Birmingham: Botanical Gardens
Jan. 30–Feb. 8

Alaska

1979
Anchorage: University Center
Aug. 29–Oct. 9

Arizona

1976
Tuscon: Park Mall
Nov. 26–Jan. 2, 1977

1978
Tuscon: Park Mall
Aug. 12–20

1980
Phoenix: Metrocenter
Feb. 23–Mar. 2

1986
Tuscon: Park Mall
Nov. 15–Dec. 31

Arkansas

1979
Little Rock:
First United Methodist Church
May 30–June 6

1981
Fort Smith: Central Mall
Sept. 1–8

1983
Fort Smith: Central Mall
Sept. 9–20

Lawton: Central Mall
Sept. 23–Oct. 9

California

1976
San Francisco:
Stonestown Shopping Center
June 25–July 14

1978
San Diego (El Cajon): Parkway Plaza
Aug. 25–Sept. 3

Sacramento: Country Club Plaza
Sept. 12–23

Oakland (Emeryville): Ragtime Museum
Oct. 29–Nov. 6

1979
San Jose (Cupertino):
Vallco Fashion Park
Oct. 24–30

Van Nuys: Gatlin Motor Showroom
Nov. 2–18

1980
Glendale: Glendale Galleria
Jan. 5–21

San Diego (El Cajon): Parkway Plaza
Jan. 25–Feb. 3

1982
Riverside: Modern Living Home Show
Jan. 20–24

Carlsbad: Plaza Camino Real
Feb. 12–21

San Fernando Valley:
Modern Living Home Show
Mar. 3–7

Santa Barbara:
Modern Living Home Show
Mar. 10–14

San Mateo: Modern Living Home Show
Mar. 17–21

San Bernardino: Inland Center
Aug. 10–Sept. 3

1986
San Jose (Cupertino):
Vallco Fashion Park
Sept. 1–Oct. 10

San Bernardino: Inland Center
Oct. 15–Nov. 10

1991
Simi Valley:
Ronald Reagan Presidential Library
Nov. 4–Jan. 20, 1992

1993
Simi Valley:
Ronald Reagan Presidential Library
Nov. 15–May 1, 1994

Colorado

1976
Denver (Lakewood): Villia Italia Center
Oct. 16–26

1978
Denver (Thornton): North Valley Mall
July 26–Aug. 6

1980
Denver (Thornton): North Valley Mall
Mar. 22–30

1981
Denver: May D & F
Oct. 10–25

Connecticut
1977
Danbury: Danbury State Fair
Oct. 1–10

Delaware
1980
Wilmington: Radisson Hotel Ballroom
Sept. 22–25

District of Columbia
1975
White House Tree Lighting Ceremony
Dec. 18

Kennedy Center for Performing Arts
Dec. 20–31

1977
Capital Center Sports Complex
July 1–10

1980
Union Station
Sept. 30–Oct. 26

1992
National Museum of American History,
Smithsonian Institution
Feb. 10–Oct. 14

Florida
1975
Orlando: Central Florida Fair
Feb. 23–Mar. 6

Orlando: Orlando Fashion Square Mall
July 1–30

Tallahassee: Tallahassee Mall
Sept. 1–18

1976
Palm Beach:
Henry Morrison Flagler Museum
Jan. 2–11

Merritt Island: Merritt Square Mall
Jan. 13–25

Daytona Beach:
Museum of Arts & Sciences
Nov. 26–Jan. 2, 1977

1977
Palm Beach:
Henry Morrison Flagler Museum
Jan. 5–16

1978
Mary Esther: Santa Rosa Mall
Jan. 11–Feb. 2

Orlando: Orlando Fashion Square Mall
Feb. 15–26

1979
Clearwater: Countryside Mall
Jan. 11–24

Jacksonville: Regency Square
Jan. 25–Feb. 4

Orlando: Orlando Fashion Square Mall
Feb. 8–20

1980
Orlando: Special Christmas Showing
Nov. 25–Dec. 30

1983
Fort Meyers: Edison Mall
Jan. 6–Feb. 3

Tampa: Florida State Fair
Feb. 9–24

Miami: Dade County Fair
Mar. 11–23

Lakeland: All American Fair
Nov. 15–26

Tampa: IBS Home Show,
Florida State Fair
Nov. 28–Dec. 3

Miami: IBS Home Show,
Miami Beach Convention Center
Dec. 7–20

1984
Fort Meyers: Edison Mall
Jan. 3–21

West Palm Beach: South Florida Fair
Jan. 26–Feb. 5

Tampa: Florida State Fair
Feb. 10–25

1985
Palm Beach: South Florida Fair
Jan. 23–Feb. 2

Tampa: Florida State Fair
Feb. 12–17

Orlando: Orlando Fashion Square Mall
Apr. 1–30

Daytona: Daytona Mall
Nov. 15–Dec. 30

1986
Fort Meyers: Edison Mall
Jan. 3–12

Palm Beach: South Florida Fair
Jan. 8–Feb. 2

Tampa: Florida State Fair
Feb. 5–16

Bushnell: Sumter County Fair
Mar. 5–16

1987
Fort Meyers: Edison Mall
Jan. 3–Feb. 1

1988
Tampa: Florida State Fair
Feb. 4–15

1990
Orlando: Marriott World Resort Center
(special showing for President Reagan)
Sept. 27

Miami Beach: Convention Center
December

1992
Miami Beach: Convention Center
June 19–29

Georgia
1975
Atlanta: International Shopping
Center Convention
Sept. 20–23

Atlanta: Lenox Square Shopping Center
Sept. 25–Oct. 5

Savannah: Oglethorpe Mall
Oct. 7–26

1977
Atlanta: Lenox Square Shopping Center
Jan. 19–30

1988
Atlanta: Lenox Square Shopping Center
July 4–Aug. 1

Hawaii
1978
Honolulu: Ala Moana Center
Oct. 3–17

Idaho
1979
Coeur d'Alene: North Shore
Convention Center
Aug. 13–18

Illinois
1976
Chicago (Lombard): Yorktown
Shopping Center
Feb. 18–29

Rockford: Cherry Vale Mall
Mar. 3–8

Sterling: Northland Mall
June 8–20

Chicago (Orland Park):
Orland Square Mall
Sept. 21–26

1977
Chicago (Aurora): Fox Valley Center
Mar. 23–29

1978
Chicago (Lombard):
Yorktown Shopping Center
Mar. 30–Apr. 9

Evergreen Park: Evergreen Plaza
June 3–21

1979
Rockford: Cherry Vale Mall
Mar. 7–11

1980
Waukegan: Lakehurst Mall
Mar. 16–25

Springfield:
Illinois Building, Illinois State Fair
Aug. 6–17

1981
Peru: Peru Mall
May 14–20

Normal: College Hills Mall
May 23–31

Dixon: Chamber of Commerce
sponsored
June 20–28

Mt. Prospect: Randhurst
Shopping Center
July 4–11

1982
Chicago:
Stratford Square Shopping Center
Sept. 10–Oct. 1

Rockford: North Town Mall
Nov. 1–15

Freeport: Lincoln Mall
Nov. 22–Dec. 31

1983
Chicago (Orland Park):
Orland Square Mall
July 20–Aug. 11

Naperville (Chicago): Fox Valley Center
Aug. 15–Sept. 3

1984
Bloomingdale: Statford Square Mall
July 19–29

Chicago (Aurora): Fox Valley Center
Aug. 3–12

Chicago (Orland Park):
Orland Square Mall
Aug. 18–26

1985
Matteson: Lincoln Mall
Aug. 23–Sept. 21

1986
Vernon Hills: Hawthorn Center
May 9–18

Joliet: Louis–Joliet Mall
May 23–June 6

Rolling Meadows:
Algonquin Mills Mall
June 10–25

1987
Deerbrook: Deerbrook Mall
May 18–26

Arlington Heights: Randhurst Mall
June 1–21

Chicago: Stratford Square
Aug. 5–9

Chicago (Aurora): Fox Valley Center
Aug. 12–16

Chicago (Orland Park):
Orland Square Mall
Aug. 19–23

Joliet: Louis–Joliet Mall
Aug. 26–30

1991
Chicago (Matteson): Lincoln Mall
May 1–June 2

Chicago Ridge: Chicago Ridge Mall
June 7–16

Skokie: Old Orchard Mall
June 21–July 28

Indiana
1976
Fort Wayne: Southtown Mall
Apr. 6–11

Terre Haute: Honey Creek Square
May 4–10

Indianapolis: Washington Square
May 13–June 1

1977
LaFayette:
Market Square Shopping Center
Mar. 16–20

1981
Lafayette:
Market Square Shopping Center
Mar. 26–Apr. 1

Elkhart: Concord Mall
June 2–10

1984
South Bend: South Bend Home Show
May 18–28

Elkhart: Concord Mall
June 2–10

Iowa
1976
Des Moines: Merle Hay Mall
Mar. 20–27

1981
Des Moines: Iowa State Fair
Aug. 13–23

Kansas
1980
Wichita: Old Downtown Train Station
Apr. 10–15

Kentucky
1977
Louisville: Oxmoor Center
June 4–11

1981
Ft. Knox (Radcliff):
Golden Armour Festival
Sept. 22–27

1986
Somerset: Somerset Mall
July 1–13

1987
Florence: Florence Mall
June 25–July 5

1989
Florence: Florence Mall
Oct. 10–Nov. 1

Louisiana
1979
New Orleans: The Plaza in Lake Forest
Apr. 27–May 5

1981
Shreveport: Expo '81 Ark–La–Tex
Home and Garden Show
Feb. 26–Mar. 1

1986
Shreveport: Expo '86 Ark–La–Tex
Home and Garden Show
Feb. 20–26

Monroe: Ark–La–Miss Home and
Recreation Show
Apr. 3–6

1987
New Orleans:
New Orleans Convention Center
Nov. 5–10

Maine
1980
Waterville: Waterville Armory
June 25–29

Maryland
1978
Baltimore:
Garden Clubs Show, State Fairgrounds
Apr. 27–May 7

Massachusetts
1977
Boston: Massachusetts Horticultural
Society
Apr. 30–May 8

Framingham: Framingham Armory
May 11–16

1992–93
Boston: John F. Kennedy Library
Nov. 15–Nov. 1, 1993

1994
Springfield:
Big Eastern Exhibition Grounds
Sept. 16–Oct. 4

Michigan
1976
Grand Rapids: Eastbrook Mall
Aug. 24–29

1977
Kalamazoo: Kalamazoo Center
June 13–19

1978
Detroit: Homebuilders Show, Cobo Hall
Mar. 14–26

1980
Holland: Dow Center for Tulip Time
Festival
May 13–19

1981
Detroit: Homebuilders Show, Cobo Hall
Mar. 14–22

1983
Detroit: Homebuilders Show, Cobo Hall
Mar. 28–Apr. 6

Jackson: Jackson County Fair
July 3–16

1984
Detroit: Homebuilders Show, Cobo Hall
Mar. 17–25

Pontiac: Summit Mall
May 18–28

1985
Jackson: Michigan County Fair
Aug. 4–10

Minnesota
1976
Minneapolis (Edina): Southdale Center
July 20–25

1981
St. Paul (Roseville): Rosedale Center
July 14–20

Hibbing: Irongate Mall
July 24–27

Willmar: Kandi Mall
July 29–Aug. 1

Worthington: Northland Mall
Aug. 26–29

1991
St. Paul: Minnesota State Fair
Aug. 21–Sept. 3

Mississippi

1975
Biloxie: Edgewater Shopping Center
Nov. 18–Dec. 6

1981
Jackson: Metrocenter
Feb. 12–21

1986
Natchez: Natchez Mall
Mar. 26–31

Missouri

1976
Columbia: Biscayne Mall
Mar. 30–Apr. 3

St. Louis: Crestwood Plaza
Apr. 13–17

St. Louis: Chesterfield Mall
Sept. 28–Oct. 2

1979
Joplin: Northpark Mall
June 11–16

Kansas City: Crown Center
June 29–July 8

1986
Columbia: Central Missouri Home,
Garden and Recreation Show
Mar. 20–23

St. Louis: Plaza Frontenac
Apr. 10–16

1987
St. Louis: Plaza Frontenac
Sept. 4–13

Montana

1979
Billings: Rimrock Mall
Aug. 2–8

Nebraska

1978
Lincoln: Gateway Mall
June 24–July 4

Omaha: Westroads Shopping Center
July 8–18

1986
Omaha: Westroads Shopping Center
Aug. 16–24

Nevada

1980
Las Vegas: Boulevard Mall
Feb. 9–17

New Hampshire

1977
Manchester: The Mall of New
Hampshire
Oct. 26–Jan. 8, 1978

New Jersey

1977
Paramus: Garden State Plaza
Apr. 2–23

1985
Cherryvale: New Jersey State Fair
July 19–29

1986
Garden State Park:
New Jersey State Fair
Aug. 1–10

1988
Garden State Park:
New Jersey State Fair
Aug. 15–25

New Mexico

1980
Albuquerque: Winrock Center
Mar. 7–16

New York

1976
Syracuse: New York State Fair
Aug. 31–Sept. 6

1977
Uniondale (Long Island):
Nassau Coliseum
Mar. 5–13
Commack (Long Island):
Commack Arena
July 16–21

Buffalo: Erie County Savings and Loan
Aug. 5–20

Brooklyn: Kings Plaza
Oct. 13–23

1978
Rochester: Midtown Plaza
May 12–27

1980
Troy: Saratoga Performing Arts Field
House
July 3–12

North Carolina

1980
Greensboro: Carolina Circle Mall
Aug. 22–31

1981
Durham: South Square Mall
Jan. 5–11

North Dakota

1979
Bismark: Northbook Mall
July 23–28

Ohio

1976
Cleveland: Parmatown Shopping Center
Apr. 27–May 2

Toledo: Lucust Fair
Aug. 3–8

Cincinnati: Northgate Mall
Sept. 9–13

1977
Cincinnati: Northgate Mall
Sept. 10–28

1978
Akron: Chapel Hill Mall
Apr. 12–17

1981
Niles: Eastwood Mall
Apr. 5–11

Tiffin: Tiffin Mall
Apr. 24–29

1987
North Randall: Randall Park Mall
July 23–30

Oklahoma
1976
Oklahoma City: Shepherd Mall
Oct. 5–12

1980
Oklahoma City: Shepherd Mall
Apr. 19–May 7

1981
Lawton: Central Mall
Sept. 11–17

1983
Oklahoma City: Shepherd Mall
Oct. 15–Nov. 9

1984
Oklahoma City: Oklahoma State Fair
Sept. 21–30

1991
Oklahoma City: Oklahoma State Fair
Sept. 13–29

Oregon
1978
Portland: Meier & Frank Company
Nov. 11–19

Pennsylvania
1977
Hazelton: Laurel Mall
May 20–30

1981
Williamsport: Downtown
Apr. 15–20

Greensburg: Greengate Mall
May 4–10

1984
Reading: Fairgrounds Square Mall
June 16–24

Johnstown: Richmond Mall
June 30–July 7

1986
Lancaster: Guernsey Pavilion Building
July 18–27

1989
Pittsburgh:
Kauffman's Department Store
Nov. 20–Dec. 31

Rhode Island
1977
Providence: Preservation Society Benefit
Feb. 24–Mar. 2

South Carolina
1979
Myrtle Beach: Myrtle Square Mall
Feb. 24–Mar. 3

South Dakota
1979
Sioux Falls: Western Mall
July 13–18

1981
Sioux Falls: Western Mall
Aug. 4–9

Tennessee
1979
Nashville: National Guard Armory
Mar. 30–Apr. 6

Memphis: Overton Square Mall
Apr. 12–22

1984
Knoxville: Tennessee Valley Fair
Sept. 3–15

1985
Knoxville: Tennessee Valley Fair
Sept. 6–14

1987
Nashville: Tennessee State Fair
Sept. 16–30

1988
Nashville: Tennessee State Fair
Sept. 18–Oct. 2

1989
Nashville: Tennessee State Fair
Sept. 15–29

1990
Knoxville: Tennessee Valley Fair
Sept. 7–17

Texas
1975
Lufkin: Angelina Mall
Nov. 10–16

1981
Texarkana: Central Mall
Mar. 3–9

Amarillo: Civic Center
Oct. 30–Nov. 8

Ft. Worth: Texas Girls Choir Building
Nov. 13–22

1984
Houston: Deerbrook Mall
Oct. 5–28

Ft. Worth: Texas Girls Choir Building
Nov. 2–17

Lufkin: Angelina Mall
Nov. 23–Dec. 30

Utah
1976
Salt Lake City: University Mall
Oct. 30–Nov. 7

Vermont
1980
Burlington: Fletcher Free Library
July 16–22

Virginia
1980
Richmond: Science Museum of Virginia
Sept. 3–14

1988
Richmond: Miller & Rhoads
Department Store
Sept. 1–14

Washington
1979
Spokane: Armory
Aug. 22–26

Seattle: Southcenter
Oct. 13–20

West Virginia

1980
Wheeling: Civic Center
July 26–Aug. 2

1987
Bluefield: Mercer Mall
July 10–19

Wisconsin

1976
Milwaukee: Mayfair Mall
Mar. 11–17

Oshkosh: Park Plaza Mall
July 27–Aug. 1

Milwaukee: Wisconsin State Fair
Aug. 12–22

Monroe: Cheese Days Festival
Sept. 16–19

1982
Beloit: Beloit Mall
Oct. 5–20

1983
Oshkosh: Park Plaza Mall
June 2–30

Jackson: Jackson County Fair
July 3–16

1986
Fond du Lac: College Gymnasium
Apr. 21–27

Monroe: West Mall
May 1–5

1987
Green Bay: Green Bay Convention
Center
Nov. 15–Jan. 1, 1988

1991
Milwaukee: Wisconsin State Fair
Aug. 1–11

Wyoming

1980
Cheyenne: Laramie Community College
Apr. 2–6

Outside the United States

1982
Madurodam, De Haag, Holland
Mar. 29–July 7

London, England: Earl's Court
(Queen's Royal Tournament)
July 14–31

1994
Tokyo Bay, Japan: Chiba City
(American Festival Japan '94)
July 6–August 29

Home of the White House Replica

The permanent home of the White
House in Miniature is the House of Presidents, 123 N. Highway 27, Clermont,
Florida 34712-0885 (exit #1, Florida
Turnpike). Open every day of the year
except Christmas, visitors are offered
the opportunity to tour the replica and
Oval Offices, visit the workshops where
craftspeople are making the miniature
furniture and accessories, see 42 lifesize
wax presidential figures, and learn the
history of the White House and the
Zweifel's recreation. For information
about the replica, other Zweifel exhibits,
and tour schedules, write the House of
Presidents or telephone (904) 394-2836.

Letters from Presidents and First Ladies

THE WHITE HOUSE
WASHINGTON

January 12, 1977

Dear Mr. Zweifel:

During the past year, Americans throughout
the country have become more aware of our
heritage because of the Bicentennial and
through the many meaningful programs and
projects which have taken place.

The "White House in Miniature", which
you have created, has been one of the
very exciting projects to have emerged.
By taking your "White House" to the people
of the nation and displaying so exact
a duplication of this national treasure,
you have given Americans throughout the
country the chance to see what so many
visitors to Washington have had the opportunity to enjoy.

My compliments to you and your staff
on a very fine effort and one which will
continue to bring pleasure to many people
as it moves from community to community.

Sincerely,

Gerald R. Ford

Mr. John Zweifel
8967 Easterling Drive
Orlando, Florida 32811

GERALD R. FORD

September 26, 1985

Dear Mr. Zweifel and Family:

Congratulations on the Tenth Anniversary of your internationally
acclaimed White House Replica Tour. I know that over the past 10
years millions of Americans and Europeans have toured your White
House and have come to appreciate and love this "gift from the
people to the people" as a symbol of the freedom we all cherish.

Because I was privileged to be President of the United States
during our Bicentennial, Betty and I hold a special affection for
your exhibit, because it captures forever the way The White House
looked on July 4, 1976.

Once again, best wishes on this important milestone and best of
luck in your continuing task of opening The White House to the
people to whom it belongs.

Sincerely,

Gerald R. Ford

Mr. John Zweifel
The White House Replica
8967 Easterling Drive
Orlando, Florida 32819

BARBARA BUSH

November 26th 1989

Dear Mr. Zweifel.
I am still thinking about the
beautiful White House that I saw
last night. My, you have done a
wonderful thing for all the country
The darling chair from the Blue Room
will be cherished in our Family
forever!

Many many thanks —

Barbara Bush

RONALD REAGAN

Dear Visitor:

Welcome to the American White House Replica.

Nancy and I are delighted that you are visiting this exquisite model of our Nation's most prominent and historic home. We have many fond memories of our years in the White House and are so happy to be able to share it with you.

As you know, the White House truly belongs to all the people of this great Nation. This authentic model creates the monument in perfect detail, as it appeared during my administration. Even the acorns I fed to the squirrels have been reproduced in front of the Oval Office!

Enjoy your tour and God bless you.

Sincerely,

Ronald Reagan

JIMMY CARTER

March 24, 1992

To White House Replica Exhibition Visitors

Rosalynn and I are pleased to welcome you to the Replica of the White House. This is a unique opportunity to view the historical progression of the home of our nation's presidents and their families.

Anyone who has visited the White House knows the wonder of being in a place so rich with history and charm. When we lived there, we loved and appreciated its elegant beauty and attached special significance to each room in the house.

But there is no better way to experience the true spirit of the grand old mansion than to visit this astonishingly detailed replica. Its legacy is recreated from the early days of construction, through two centuries of transformation, reflecting the character and personal preferences of the families who have called it home.

During the White House 200th Birthday celebration, we hope that many people will enjoy the Zweifel's remarkable gift to their country.

Sincerely,

Jimmy Carter
Rosalynn Carter

RICHARD NIXON

577 CHESTNUT RIDGE ROAD
WOODCLIFF LAKE, NEW JERSEY

Mrs. Nixon and I always viewed the White House as the People's House, which is why, as First Lady, Mrs. Nixon threw its doors and gardens open to more people than ever before. Now, through the precise detail of John Zweifel's extraordinary model, even more people can experience the warmth, beauty, and history of the White House.

Richard Nixon
2-10-92

Stonewall, Texas

March 25, 1992

Dear Friends,

As you 'tour' the White House through the magic of this fascinating replica, I hope you will pause and reflect on the story of this beloved home.

Perhaps you will be led to travel back though time and think about the exciting saga of America -- the lives of our leaders and the history they have written within these walls. I hope, too, you will think about the families who have occupied it and added another dimension to the legacy of the President's House.

With all good wishes,

Sincerely,

Lady Bird Johnson

Notes

1 William Seale, *The President's House: A History*, 2 vols. (Washington, D.C.: White House Historical Association, with the cooperation of the National Geographic Society, 1986), 1:320.

2 Ibid, p. 474.

3 *The White House: An Historic Guide* (Washington, D.C.: White House Historical Association, with the cooperation of the National Geographic Society, 1982), p. 19.

4 Margaret Brown Klapthor, *Official White House China: 1789 to the Present* (Washington, D.C.: Smithsonian Institution Press, 1975), p. 61.

5 Seale, *The President's House,* 1:95.

6 Ibid, 2:935–36.

7 William Kloss, *A Nation's Pride* (Washington, D.C.: White House Historical Association, in cooperation with the National Geographic Society, 1992), p. 143.

8 Seale, *The President's House,* 1:108.

9 Margaret Klapthor and Dione Lucas, *The First Ladies Cook Book* (New York: Parents Magazine Enterprises, 1982), p. 64.

10 Irwin Hood Hoover, *Forty-two Years in the White House* (Boston: Houghton Mifflin, 1934), p. 3.

11 Elise K. Kirk, *Musical Highlights from the White House* (Malabar, Fla.: Krieger, 1992), p. 92.

12 Seale, *The President's House,* 2:999.

13 Ibid, 2:987.

14 Perry Wolff, *A Tour of the White House with Mrs. John F. Kennedy* (Garden City, N.Y.: Doubleday, 1962), pp. 231–32.

15 *Life* (September 1, 1961), p.65.

16 Hoover, *Forty-two Years in the White House,* p. 153.

17 Philip B. Kunhardt Jr., Philip B. Kunhardt III, and Peter W. Kunhardt, *Lincoln* (New York: Knopf, 1992), p. 278.

18 Seale, *The President's House,* 1:406.

19 Wolff, *A Tour of the White House with Mrs. John F. Kennedy,* p. 10.